INTERCESSION CITY "LIVES AGAIN"

ENGLAND HALL — INTERCESSION CITY, FLA.

Jack & Donna **Wesley Weaver**

Be Blessed by God's Story
of His City!

Wesley Weaver

Self-published by: Rise-Up ONE UNITED VOICE, Inc. PO Box 1073
Intercession City, FL 33848 www.intercessioncityliveagain.org

RESOURCES: Historic Intercession City website by T. J. Lavigne:
http://www.historicintercessioncity.com

The Book of Osie or The Life of Bishop Osie England by
Clarence Allison Maddy

Defender of the Faith publication, December 1923, Osie England

The Charlie Bulldog Wireman Story:
http://www.thefinalharvest.org/online%20books/lovingatheists/bulldog.htm

Images and writings contributed by Wesley J. and Arabella A. Weaver including
photos from Lawrence Weaver's photo album (The author's father).

Interviews and information collected from various individuals having
knowledge of Intercession City.

Scripture quotations are taken from the New King James Version.
Copyright © 1982 by Thomas Nelson, Inc. All rights reserved. The views
expressed within the contents of this book are of the author and contributors
of Intercession City Lives Again and may or may not reflect those connected to
the establishment of Intercession City including the church leaders and their
families, i.e., The Household of Faith, The Wesleyan Methodist Church, The
Pilgrim Holiness Church, and The Wesleyan Church.

Wesley and Arabella Weaver are available for speaking engagements.
Email us at oneunitedvoicefl@gmail.com.

ISBN: 978-1-7340852-0-4 (paperback)
ISBN: 978-1-7340852-2-8 (color version paperback)
ISBN: 978-1-7340852-1-1 (ebook)

CONTENTS

Dedication

Intercession City Lives Again is dedicated in memory of T. J. Lavigne, our beloved friend, minister of the Gospel, and Christian historian—"The Historian of Intercession City." T.J., we miss you greatly! We are forever indebted to you and other forerunners who shared your vision for the rebirth of Intercession City. Thank you for laying the foundation so that Intercession City can "Live Again."

Theodore Joseph (T.J.) Lavigne
(1951-2017)

FOREWORD

By Arabella Weaver

"HISTORIC INTERCESSION CITY" then and "Intercession City Lives Again" now, both stories as only Wesley can tell them. Wesley does a matchless job with this exhaustive study and collection of Bishop Osie England and her small group of orphans that would become Intercessors, known then as the Ropeholders. Wesley's father, Lawrence Weaver, was among this group journeying from Point Pleasant, West Virginia, to establish a city of 24 hour 7 days a week prayer at four different locations that included three Prayer Cabins and the Large House of Prayer—now the Community Wesleyan Church, still remains in use today. Prayers went up day and night for thirteen years (1934 to 1947) and missionaries were sent out all over the world and at home to the First Nation. The hearts and prayers of Osie and her intercessors longed for world-wide revival. The altar rails were stained with the tears of those who cried out for lost souls. The 24/7 hours of fervent prayers of the Intercessors remind us of the 100 years of 24/7 prayers by the Moravians which produced worldwide revival and an abundant harvest throughout the world during the 1700s and 1800s The latter part of T.J. Lavigne's life was consumed with re-igniting the fires of revival, bringing back God's Glory, and preserving the legacy of this great woman of God and the City of Prayer in the heart of Florida. T.J. Lavigne's torch-light lit the way for the Rebirth of God's City as a "City of Prayer." God said, "Tell My

Intercessors to take ownership of My City, Intercession City." Once again, the stopped-up wells will flow again with revival fire not only for Intercession City, but for the State, for the Nation, and for the entire World.

On July 30, 2018, just past midnight I received the following vision: *"As Wesley began to share five smooth stones (5 Scriptures) in regard to provision (Israelites plundering the Egyptians upon their departure to the wilderness, and Cyrus's decree to the inhabitants to provide silver, gold, etc. for the rebuilding of the Temple), I was hit so strongly with a Word from God to not rent a tent, but to buy a tent. That we were to put it on the land where the prayer cabin was—where the synergy of the ages would connect. The Lord had said "Intercession City is HIS CITY and is the City for Intercessors where the Intercessors would come and intercede and pray day and night; and a Portal shall be opened as a Well, and the Well would be the Portal." "Oh God! I see it! I see it! Oh, I see it!" He said, "This would be the plea to the Intercessors to give to purchase the Tent of Intercession— The TENT OF INTERCESSION."*

The weight of the assignment is so heavy that it put me on the floor. "Oh God, How? How? Oh God, How? Oh Jesus, How?" As I cried out to the Lord asking How? I heard Wesley say "God shall provide." The weight of the assignment was because I heard "100 days." "100 days." "100 days." And, I was reminded of the Conference Call on August 8th while I was awakening from rest. The Lord said, "The 100 Day Prayer Revival would come again." I knew in my spirit, but I said nothing. I said nothing because the assignment was so big. The assignment was so far beyond me. I asked the Lord as I laid on the floor: "When was the 100 Day Prayer Revival to start?" The Lord said: "His New Year." The CRY was before the Lord, because of the assignment that seems so heavy. So big! But as I asked "How?" He said, "It is not for you to carry." Bring my Twelve together—these that I instruct to call—bring together." "Share the Vision and they will bring it together." He said "12-hour shifts." Oh, My God, He said "12-hour shifts" He was showing me it would be 24 hours of prayer. Known feeling is the same that they shall feel, but I have prepared their heart and I have trained them for the assignment. While on the floor I saw the tent with lights. There was an area where Randy (Randy Law is co-pastor of Intercession City Church of God) *had the children teaching them on prayer—Raising the children to pray. I've seen her at the Wesleyan Church. I've seen where it was raining and somebody had gotten these white things and put around the tent—Like thin boards, but they were plastic and went into the ground and it kept the rain out. Then there were these flood bags that went inside where the plastic boards met to keep the water out of the tent. What was so powerful what the Lord just showed me was when He said that the Portal* (Well) *He told me about inviting the people in for the 100 Day Revival. I told you* (Wesley) *it would be the connections that would rebuild Intercession City. Remember the picture Karen* (Karen Ledbetter) *painted last year of the Well? That is a Portal! The Lord showed me that the Well would be shooting out* (gushing out) *like dirt and stuff. The difference was the Well she painted last year had all these shoots coming out of it—Bright colors that looked like sparks coming out like stars, and they were going around the world. Like God put a stick of dynamite in the Well and shoots up like fireworks going counter-clockwise. You could hear it like rocks being torn—rumbling sounds like taking a huge big drill and drilling into the ground, breaking up rock—breaking up hard rock from the ground.* (Sparks) *One to South America, One to Africa, One to the United Kingdom, One to Iceland, Greenland and Canada, One to Hawaii—All around the world. Some went so far you could not see where they went.*

Praise God! Again, this was the beginning of a Movement. The Sparks of Revival touching down All over the world, from state, to nation, to continent and around the world. Father has instructed us to have 24/7—100 Day Prayer Revival, because it's all about souls being saved, man reconciled back to God, the Creator of Heaven and Earth, the Land in Unity with His Creation Again. Since Osie England came in obedience, built in obedience, but among other things left because "she grew weary in well doing"…the land has continued to groan for redemption. Father chooses the heart of Florida to call His Intercessors to intercede His perfect will. Will we answer the 24/7—100 Day Prayer that prepares the way for Revival of the church and lost souls? Are we willing to make the sacrifice, to lay aside all our idols and follow Christ? No true Revival has ever come without fervent intercession and can only remain in constant repentance of dis-unity. Creation was made to be one with each other and one with Father—our Creator. John 17, Jesus is very clear—the only way the world will see and know Father's Son is in their oneness, their unity; because, the world sees their Creator, what they had been looking for since birth. Intercede Heaven into the Earth… Worldwide Revival…Reconcile man back to Father…His Kingdom Come and will be done…Back to the Garden… *You will see as you read that there will be some passages or graphics that say, "Intercession City Live Again" and other places "Intercession City Lives Again". During the 24/7—100 DAY Prayer Revival, the revelation came forth that Intercession City Lives NOW! …and thus the differences.

Painting by Karen Ledbetter at the Feast of Tabernacles Oct. 6-7, 2017 Intercession City, FL

100-Day 24-hour Prayer, Revival Announced (Arabella's Vision)

INTRODUCTION

THERE HAS BEEN A NUMBER OF PROPHECIES, dreams and visions of Florida being a Forerunner State. A Forerunner is a predecessor, ancestor, forebear, precursor. The word Forerunner is a prophetic statement, or indication of something to follow. John the Baptist was a Forerunner. He was sent in advance to announce the coming of Jesus as our Savior. We believe Florida will be the leading state God will use to lead Revival Awakening for the Nation and around the World. Apostle Chuck Pierce prophesied that Florida is developing a backbone in its center. We believe Intercession City (The very center of Florida) is a part of that backbone.

Why Florida? Until a couple of years ago I did not know the extent of Intercessory Prayer in Florida. History will teach us that before there is revival in any area there is intercessory prayer. I recall for two and one half years there were fervent, persistent prayers by the church members of Brownsville Assembly of God Church in Pensacola, Florida interceding day and night for Revival ushering in the Brownsville Revival of which I had the privilege of being a part of for seven years and served as the Accountant for the Revival. The prayer movement in Florida is phenomenal. The state is saturated with prayer warriors. The very center of Florida, Intercession City, was once a city of 24 hours, seven days a week City of Prayer that lasted for thirteen years. In fact, Intercession City received its name from the small group of intercessors who miraculously found the place through fasting and intercessory prayer in 1934. Osie England and her small group from Point

Pleasant, West Virginia traveled to Apopka, Florida looking for a place for her orphanage. Down to only 70 cents, an all day and all-night time of prayer and fasting was called by Osie England. During this time of intercessory prayer God showed them Interocean City only 40 miles south of their camp ground. They met with the owner and was given the entire city with 5,000 acres for only $100,000 worth at that time one million dollars.

The purpose of this book entitled *Intercession City Lives Again* is to tell the story of God's City. God said, "Tell My Story about My City called Intercession City". He wants His City back. He is calling intercessors throughout the State to take ownership of His City, the Spiritual Capital of Florida, and to Intercede for Revival not only for the State of Florida but for the Nation and the World.

1

ORIGIN OF INTERCESSION CITY

MANY PEOPLE ASK, "Is there really a place called Intercession City?" You will not readily find it on the map, but if you zoom down far enough you will find this small community between Old Tampa Highway and South Orange Blossom Trail about seven miles southwest of Kissimmee, Florida and twelve miles southeast of Disney World. It was not always called Intercession City, nor was it always small. The original dream was that of Mr. J.W. White, a millionaire promoter from the North who started building his dream city called "Interocean City" in 1923. Named Interocean for its location of half way between the Atlantic and Gulf waters, it was a massive project that included a beautiful resort hotel, buildings, streets, houses, farms, orchards, lakes and entertainment, including aquatic amphitheaters, golfing, fishing, hunting, motoring, yachting and a casino that would be the Las Vegas of the South. He had plans to connect the Florida Gulf Coast and Atlantic Ocean by waterways, to his Interocean City so that boats could travel inland. It was a resort and entertainment project that would have dwarfed present day Disney World. Ironically this 5,000-acre project adjoins Disney World to the north built in 1971. Mr. White was definitely a man ahead of his time. An army of workmen converged on White's vast prairie and by the onset of the 1924-25 winter season, the Interocean City Hotel was finished at a cost of $300,000. He went on to build and sell $200,000 worth of homes, with sidewalks and streets. Today's value would have been in the millions.

But God had something else in mind. He wanted this city located in the very heart of Florida to be the spiritual capital of this great State of Florida—"The Jerusalem of Florida—God's City." God Himself wanted to be the main attraction, the heartbeat of the Father in the very heart of Florida, not the entertainment center that Interocean City would have provided, nor its successor, Disney World, which is now the theme park capital of the world with 62 million visitors annually. Interocean City sprung up during the 1920s ("Roaring Twenties")—a decade of prosperity in North America during the economic boom following World War I. Then in 1925 it happened. The Great Depression of 1929-1939 brought the building of Mr. J.W. White's Interocean City resort to a screeching halt. The workers arrived at Interocean City for their paychecks, only to find that the boss men weren't around. It was never completed because the developer fell on hard times prior to the 1929 Stock Market crash. Mr. J.W. (John Wesley) Wile, former owner of the 5,000 acres, sold it to J.W. White and then repossessed the entire bankrupted Interocean City project. Interocean City sat idle and became known as "Florida's Biggest Ghost Town" for 10 years. The magnificent hotel stood vacant for a decade like a medieval castle on an empty plain. Cattle chewed grass on the huge porch of the once-great hotel. The stores, office buildings, homes, lighted streets, sidewalks, millwork and truck factories became empty.

John Wesley Wile, (1866-1951)

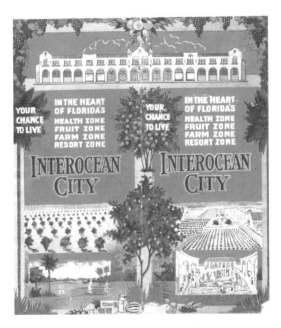

Mr. John Wesley Wile was the Owner of the 5,000 acres of land sold to J. W. White, developer of Interocean City which failed. It was repossessed by Mr. Wile and later sold to Osie England for an orphanage.

The Interocean City Hotel under construction in 1925, just before the impact of the Great Depression affected the U.S.A.

Picture taken of the Interocean City Administrative Building by Wesley's father when he arrived in 1935. This building became the Chapel, Library and Girl's Dorm for Osie England's Bible College. The buildings sat vacant for ten years.

Picture of the back of the old hotel taken by Wesley's father in 1935.

Sign posted on South Orange Blossom Trail

Intercession City New Name Given To Ex-Boom Town

KISSIMMEE, Feb. 13.—(Special.)—Interocean City, million-dollar boomtime development six miles south of here which faded into a ghost town after collapse of the boom, will be known as Intercession City hereafter.

The Household of Faith, an Evangelical Christian belief with missions in West Virginia, Ohio and Minnesota, whose sponsors acquired the 5000-acre town and adjoining lands in January, has requested the post office department to make the change.

Apostles of the Faith said today that "Intercession" was more in tune with the spirit of the backers of the development than "Interocean."

About 100 new residents are reported and considerable building is in progress.

Article announcing the name change from Interocean City to Intercession City.
Date: February 13, 1936

The City of Dreams!

2

GOD'S PLAN FOR THE CITY

ON NOVEMBER 24, 1934, while the Great Depression was at its worst, a group of people departed from Point Pleasant, West Virginia for Florida. Miss Osie England, the leader of the group, was accompanied by one of her former students, Mr. Clarence Maddy and others. Mr. Maddy suggested that due to the cold winters and the expense of heat they should go south to a warmer climate and locate a winter home. Orphanage workers and 40 orphans were loaded into 2 trucks and several cars. The group arrived at Apopka, Florida approximately 20 miles northwest of Orlando and set up camp at a Tourist Court. Mr. Maddy began his search for a suitable place to settle. As mentioned in the Introduction the situation turned for the worst when Miss Osie announced that they were down to 70 cents. Before her announcement Osie had spent many nights in prayer when she was down to her last dollar. An all day and all-night time of intercessory prayer and fasting was initiated. Desperate people in a desperate situation prayed all night and the Lord answered with a vision of where to go. During the time of prayer and fasting Mr. Maddy had a vision of a large place with spacious buildings on it. Osie England and Clarence Maddy immediately began their search for the place described in his vision. They did not have to go far. Interocean City was just 40 miles south, located seven miles southwest of Kissimmee, Florida on Old Tampa Highway and South Orange Blossom Trail. It was the location of the former boom town that had fallen prey to the stock market crash of 1929. It consisted of several buildings including a hotel, an apartment building, an administration building, about 6 residences, and other unfinished buildings. According to Edgar Wyant (one of the orphans that accompanied Osie England from West Virginia in 1934) the 5,000-acre tract included land between what is now Highway 192 (W. Irlo Bronson Memorial Hwy.) and Old Dixie Highway (Now Old Tampa Hwy) and across the railroad tracks back almost to where the Disney-owned property and Celebration are today. It also included some of what is now Campbell City, and all of the land which is now Good Samaritan Village (North side of S. Orange Blossom Trail and West of Pleasant Hill Road including a large frontage on Lake Tohopekaliga). Mr. Maddy located the owner, a Mr. John Wesley Wile of Kissimmee, Florida and was able to obtain the property at one tenth of its value for $100,000 which included 5,000 acres of land with generous terms of no down payment under an annuity payment arrangement. A Miracle of its time by no stretch of the imagination. This same land today between Kissimmee and Celebration is worth millions. God's favor was definitely upon Ms. Osie England and her penniless humble party from West Virginia! When $50,000 of the mortgage was paid, Mr. Wile gave the school a clear title to the property for the remaining $50,000. The plan was to establish an orphanage and they applied for a license to the State of Florida. The state inspectors found the buildings unsatisfactory for an orphanage and denied the license. So, in the spring of 1935, everyone returned to Point Pleasant, leaving 5 adults and 7 youth to maintain the property.

Miss Rudd and Miss Cox remained in Intercession City. With practically no help from Point Pleasant, they were forced to "fend for themselves." They went to the canal at Campbell Station and caught fish. In the fields they picked huckleberries, with which they made pies. The road through Interocean City was very rough and often food stuff fell from the trucks passing through. One time, several crates of grapefruit were found and on another occasion several hampers of green beans. The cooks longed for cheese but there was no money. Their prayers were answered when a wheel of cheese fell off a passing truck just in front of the administration building. Miss Rudd tried to chase down the truck but to no avail. Macaroni and cheese made a big hit with everyone.

On each Saturday night, Miss Rudd took out a group for street meetings. They played instruments, sang, and Miss Rudd preached. The Lord put it upon the heart of a Mr. Thomas in St. Cloud to furnish meat. He never failed to provide meat for Sunday dinner. They acquired bantam hens from which eggs were collected to make banana pudding for Sunday dessert. In 1935 when Osie England and others who accompanied her (including my father, Lawrence Weaver) returned to Interocean City, a contest was offered to give an appropriate name to Interocean City, the prize being a house lot worth about $200.00. The winner suggested "Intercession City" (from their incessant prayers) and the name was officially changed from Interocean City to Intercession City, known as the City of Prayer. A Post Office was established with Miss Cox as Postmaster and Miss Rudd as Mail Carrier. The mail was picked up each day at Kissimmee. All monies from these jobs were put into the general fund. In 1939 a monthly paper named "The Defender of the Faith" was published by Mr. Maddy. The Publishing House (Intercession City Publishing House for the W. Va. Training School) was one of the largest and most complete of any Gospel Publishing House. Each month, the great 16-page Gospel Magazine, "The Defender of the Faith", was distributed to over 32,000 persons in the United States and many foreign countries.

During the fall of 1939 Dr. A.J. Smith and his family arrived to start a Bible College. It was called Intercession City Bible College (ICBC) and started in October 1939. During the winter of 1942-1943, Miss Osie England started the 100 Day Revival Meetings. The first meetings were only one (1) service a day at 7 pm. The 100 Day Revival Meetings started on December 1st and went every day thru March 15th. In the latter years the 100 Day meetings were three (3) services a day and started in the first week of January with well-known evangelists preaching. Many gifted preachers from various denominations and singers came from all parts of the country. One notable minister was Dr. Henry Clay Morrison, president of Asbury College for many years and instrumental in founding Asbury Theological Seminary. This great Methodist Evangelist was regarded to be the greatest pulpit orator on the American Continent. He was editor of the widely read Pentecostal Herald. Dr. Morrison and his wife visited Intercession City quite often and even preached in the 100 Day Revival Camp Meetings held each Winter.

Many people came to know the Lord Jesus Christ as their personal Savior. It was said that you could hear them praying and shouting on the streets of Intercession City at 3 am in the morning. Intercession City was growing with restaurants, trailer park, general store, service stations, etc. The *Book of Osie* states: "... *the town of Interocean, which was merely a wide place in the road covered with dilapidated buildings, has become, as it were, the religious capital of Florida known as Intercession City, the Miracle City. A man who was traveling towards this point asked a porter on the train if he knew where Intercession City was. The porter replied, 'Yes, Lawd, it is the 'growinest' town in this country.'"* And yes, during her glory days Intercession City was indeed outpacing her twin city, Kissimmee.

Intercession City, "The City of Prayer" and "The Golden Rule Town", became one of the most beautiful and peaceful towns in the United States. There was no need for jails or law enforcement to keep the peace. No beer, alcohol, cigarettes, or gambling were allowed in town. It was His City (God's Colony). The following is an account given of Intercession City by Pastor James Kreider who pastored the Wesleyan Church in Intercession City:

In the mid-940s, "100-Day Camp Meetings" came to the community. Revival services were held during the winter. "My mother visited her parents during one of the camp meetings. Evangelists took turns preaching for 10 days, for 100 days. Each guest who came helped with the repairs and work around the school," Kreider said. Businesses began to come to Intercession City in the early 1940s, but when newcomers arrived, they soon learned they had to abide by some very strict rules. No beer, alcohol or cigarettes were allowed in town, and women were not allowed to wear shorts or slacks. In addition, each person who bought property in the community signed an agreement that he would not operate or consent to the operation of a business that sold alcoholic beverages or tobacco, or was open on Sunday. There would be no gambling devices such as pool tables, playing cards, slot machines, punchboards or raffling outfits on any of the premises. Dog owners were not allowed to let their dogs run at large. No landholder could build a church building, clubhouse or place of amusement without petitioning and getting written consent of three-fourths of the population. Within the boundary of the 5,000-acre tract, there could be no paid amusements, such as talking pictures, circuses or vaudeville, unless they had been approved as having educational or religious value. Anyone who violated the restrictions after he had received three notices had to cede title to his property, which automatically reverted to the school.

Twenty-four-hour prayer seven days a week went forth from three different locations in Intercession City (Two Cabins and the Music Emporium), not to mention the church which was called the "Large House of Prayer." It was said that the altar rails were stained with the tears of the intercessors crying out for a world of lost souls. Intercession City was indeed a city of intercessors and the only city in the United States and perhaps the world named after intercessory prayer and intercessors. You could walk down any of the streets of this city known as *The City of Prayer* and hear prayers coming from the windows of most every home. During the night season you could hear shouts from the streets as late as 3 am in the mornings. Today

God is calling the intercessors back to His City from all over the State of Florida to pray and intercede the perfect Will of the Father not only for the City but for the nation and the world. Many of these prayer warriors were called "Ropeholders" because they held up in prayer, night and day, those who were sent out to the mission field. It is the belief of this group that "holding the ropes" by mean of intercessory prayer is an important part of missionary work. "We of the group intend to be 'Ropeholder Missionaries' until we hear the command, 'Go ye.'" And "Go ye" they did. They went by the dozens by ships with their meager belongings: To East Africa, to South Africa, to Cuba, to Egypt, to Ethiopia, to Haiti, to India, to New Guinea and many other places around the world. Some were martyred. On the home front missionaries were sent to the American Indians. The 24/7 Intercessory Prayer from the prayer cabins in Intercession City was taking a toll on the Kingdom of Darkness. A worldwide revival was about to take place. Excerpt from "The Book of Osie" or "The Life of Bishop Osie England." Page 53 (2nd and 4th paragraph).

History teaches that every great revival or religious reform has come about by extraordinary agony and burden-bearing. Miss Osie has likely shed more tears over incorrigible students, prodigal boys and girls and un-regenerated sinners than any other Christian woman since the days of the wailing women of Jerusalem or the time of the weeping prophet who wished that his head were rivers and his eyes fountains of water that he might weep day and night for those who were perishing without salvation...The type of crying and weeping in which Miss England so often engages is not for self-pity for sentimental reasons, but the type of weeping that Jesus did as He approached Jerusalem and the tomb of Lazarus. When the reader can show the writer more burden-bearers who prevail in tears for lost souls, then he can show you a revival of worldwide proportion for which our generation has so often hoped and prayed.

I believe the prayers of Miss Osie and her Intercessors for a "revival of world-wide proportion" which they so often hoped and prayed for as mentioned above was cut short and should have continued. However, 70 years later after my return to Intercession City, those prayers and tears have been stored in Heaven and the bowl is about to be tipped over with Holy Fire. The cloud of witnesses is cheering us on. Let the Fire burn in Intercession City again and spread like wildfire throughout Florida, the United States and the uttermost parts of the world. Millions more to be reached now than then. Some Things Said About Intercession City:

INTERCESSION CITY IS THE:

CITY OF PRAYER

A NEW JERUSALEM

CITY OF DESTINY

THE JERUSALEM OF FLORIDA

CITY OF DREAMS

RELIGIOUS CAPITAL OF FLORIDA

GOD'S COLONY

SPIRITUAL CENTER OF THE WORLD

GATEWAY CITY

FIVE-FOLD TRAINING CENTER

GOLDEN RULE TOWN

HOME TO A COMPANY OF PROPHETS

MIRACLE CITY

THE HEART OF FLORIDA

ZION

Source: Defender of the Faith Magazine, The Book of Osie England, & other sources)

Bishop Osie England in pulpit 1946. Morrison Memorial Church Located on England Blvd.

The Large House of Prayer (Morrison Memorial Church)

The Large House of Prayer was named Morrison Memorial Church after the well known Methodist minister Henry Clay Morrison who preached many times during the 100 Day Revival Meetings.

In 1943, Miss Osie England started the 100 Day Revival Meetings. Here's a sign that promoted the "OLD TIME GOSPEL" meetings, that was placed in front of England Hall

Missionary Training School Missionaries were sent all over the world and to the Native Americans.

Prayer Cabins 1 & 2, on the side of the Main Hotel (England Hall).

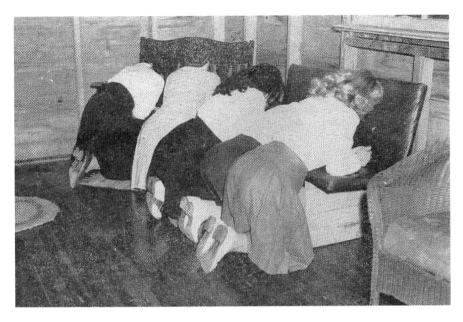

The girls in Prayer Cabin #2, used little pillows to kneel on.

The Music Emporium is where ICBC students learned how to play instruments. It was also used by students for prayer. (Prayer Cabin 3)

City of Prayer (1934–1947)

They prayed on England Blvd. on their knees and in front of the Chapel (The Administration Building)

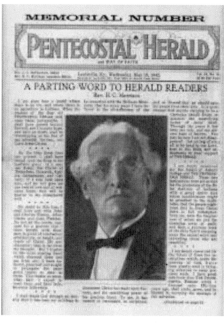

Dr. Henry Clay Morrison was a frequent visitor to Intercession City

Many well-known ministers of various denominations preached during the 100 Day Revival in Intercession City. Dr. Henry Clay Morrison is standing with his wife in front of the Chapel of the Administrative Building. Dr. Morrison and his wife visited Intercession City quite often and preached in the 100 Day Revival Meetings. He was President of Asbury College and also one of the founders of Asbury Theological Seminary. He was known as the most gifted pulpit orator in North America. Dr. Morrison was the Editor of the well-known publication, The Pentecostal Herald.

Hurricanes and fires contributed to the destruction of buildings in Intercession City.

3
ABOUT BISHOP OSIE ENGLAND

Miss Ossie England (1877-1957)
Bishop of the Household of Faith Church (Wesleyan Methodist)
Founder of Intercession City (City of Prayer)

The life of Bishop Osie England is recorded in "The Book of Osie or The Life of Bishop Osie England" by Clarence Allison Maddy. Osie, Osee or Hosea means Salvation (Romans 9:25). Osie was born April 7, 1877, in the hills of Ross County, Ohio. Her parents were Mr. and Mrs. A. W. England. Osie grew up in Chillicothe, Ohio where she attended school. At age 13 she was studying hard and was ready for high school. Her parents were unable to send her to the Chillicothe school, so she took the 8th grade work the second time. While repeating the 8th grade her teachers taught some high school subjects to her. Osie subscribed to *The Youth's Companion*, carried library books back and forth for four miles, and rented an organ for the school to give lessons to those who wanted to learn music. She studied under a private instructor and regularly attended the summer sessions at Ohio University. Miss Osie England became a school teacher and drew her first pay check one day before she turned 16 years old. Boys and girls were enrolled in her classes that were older than herself, but she wisely kept quiet about her age lest her youth have a bad effect upon the discipline of her school.

In 1900 her father, A. W. England suddenly developed pneumonia and was taken from them almost instantly. This bereavement shocked all the loved ones and especially Miss Osie. She had a nervous breakdown, accompanied by a heart ailment, traces of tuberculosis and an anemic condition and she went down to a shadow of her former self. In spite of her physical condition, Miss Osie accepted a school at Locust Point, Ohio, in order to provide support for her widowed mother and to meet debts which had been incurred by her family.

In the middle of the term a strange thing happened. A lady with her husband and three small children moved into a tenant house and placed her two little girls in the school. One eventful evening, Miss Osie, when on her way home from school, was met by the mother who asked permission for a certain minister to come to the schoolhouse and conduct a two-week's meeting. Her face glowed with a heavenly light as she told of how she had been led to the Lord through the preaching of this man. Miss Osie tried to refer the woman to the school board, but the mother replied, "I have been to the school board and they said it was just whatever you said. Miss Osie said it would be alright.

The preacher was not at all what Miss Osie expected but was sent by God for that community. The terms he used, such as, "conviction," "salvation," "restitution," "conversion," and "being saved," were all new words in the vocabulary of his congregation. The next night people began to come from every direction and some of the best people of the community began stepping out to the altar where they prayed earnestly and received a great blessing for their repentance and contrition. Soon Miss Osie's students began walking past her on their way to seek the Lord. She also went forward but without conviction. The meeting closed but the people who had become spiritually aroused by the meeting opened their homes for prayer service. On the night that special service was to be conducted from the England home, this gifted school teacher was feeling the need of a Savior as never before. When she saw the people, who lived all around them singing, shouting and praising the Lord in their newfound joy, she slipped into an adjoining bedroom and there had it out to the finish with the Lord. She vowed she would never leave the place where she was kneeling until the Lord satisfied her soul. As she was seeking earnestly, the Lord came suddenly into her heart and she never had reason to doubt her wonderful conversion.

Miss Osie quickly advanced and became Vice President of the Ohio State Teacher's Association and was getting offers of advancement from many parts of the state. She now had to make a great lasting choice to continue her success as an educator or choose the humble way of the cross. Osie chose the call of God on her life. Of all the hundreds of friends she lost in the educational field, she gained thousands for the Lord in a spiritual vineyard. If she had failed to fulfill her call, numbers would likely never have found the Lord. When the Lord called Osie out of that schoolroom, He told her that He no longer wanted her salary, which she had been very liberal with in helping the poor and needy, but He wanted her. This led her to a needy world and soon she and her co-laborers founded the West Virginia Training School in Point Pleasant, West Virginia in 1923. At this time Miss Osie was 46 years old.

The first session of the West Virginia Training School was in 1923-24, a three-month term with an enrollment of 40 boys and girls who accepted training for missionary work at home and abroad. No charge was made for board, lodging or books. Each succeeding year they had from 3 to 4 months of school. The course provided the study of the Bible, general history, Latin, English, algebra and practical nursing. In small groups the students were trained by some experienced leader to visit and minister to the sick and needy, hold street meeting and jail services. Osie England became Bishop of her organization The Household of Faith (Wesleyan Methodist) in West Virginia.

In 1934 Bishop Osie England answered the call to the Southland in search for a warmer climate for her orphanage. This part of her life is covered above. After the first year, the orphanage was moved back to Point Pleasant because the State would not issue a permit due to the condition of the building. Instead, a Bible College and Missionary Training School was established in the renovated buildings in Intercession City. A Church was built named Morrison Memorial Church and Osie England became the first Pastor. Prayer cabins and centers went up throughout the City. There was a library, chapel, dormitory, and other structures built including Osie England's home across the street from the Church which still stands today.

Rev. Clarence A. Maddy, Assistant to Bishop Osie England.
Builder and Herald of Intercession City

The Lord blessed and produced many preachers, home and foreign missionaries from this humble group. Only eternity will reveal the fruit Bishop Osie England and her followers produced from those two small towns of Point Pleasant and Intercession City. Osie England also had a heart for the elderly and had homes for the elderly in West Virginia, Florida and Kentucky. The following are a few of her many activities for the Kingdom of God:

Bible Training School

Orphanage in West Virginia

Homes for the elderly in West Virginia, Florida and Kentucky

Camp meetings in West Virginia and Florida: 100-Day Camp meetings in Intercession City

Tabernacles for Camp Meetings built in Wet Virginia at three different locations

Home and Foreign Missions training center: Missionary sending society to many countries.

Street Meetings

Prison, Hospital and Elderly visitations.

Radio Station Broadcast

Printing for 32 thousand subscribers: Defenders of the Faith publication

OSIE ENGLAND DAY

In honor of Miss Osie England, Intercession City's Founder and 1st Pastor, we are Celebrating the First Annual "Osie England Day"

Miss Osie England
April 7, 1877 - October 28, 1957

This celebration will be on her birthday, **April 7, 2015, at 1 pm**, in the **Shelby Cox Memorial Park**, next to the Post Office and fenced yard.

There will be Exhibits pertaining to the History of Intercession City as well as Live Music, Cake, Ice Cream, Lemonade and fun for all.

Please attend and share your memories as others also remind you of the precious times and seasons of prayer, worship, Revival, fellowship and work that were spent in Intercession City, as well as learning about the community's glorious beginnings, successes, hardships and struggles.

When Miss Osie and her team bought Interocean City in 1934, the decaying buildings needed much attention. Miss Osie and Mr. Maddy were like Nehemiah on the wall supervising the repairs and rebuilding the community. As they progressed, the ultimately renamed the community "Intercession City" because of the incessant **PRAYER**, which was the first thing they did.

Historian T.J. Lavigne sets aside April 7th as "Osie England Day" In honor of Miss. Osie England on her Birthday April 7th

Osie England standing in front of her home on England Blvd. across the street from the Church—
The Large House of Prayer

Osie England's Home Today

4

FALL OF INTERCESSION CITY

This is the sad part of the history of Osie England and Intercession City. What happened to Intercession City? How could this once prosperous flourishing city of intercessory prayer become one of the poorest communities in Florida? How could my father who experienced so much of God's presence in the City of Prayer turn to palm-readers and witchcraft. I shall never forget my father's words the last time I saw him when I was about five years old. He held me in his lap and said: "Son, do not ever drink or smoke." I attribute his words and being raised in a Christian home to my becoming a "Nazarite"—Never touching alcohol or tobacco, living a clean life, being a man of integrity, remaining a virgin until married, and always striving to do that which is right. Not that this made me righteous—I am only righteous through the shed blood of Jesus and the forgiveness of my sins. But, this allowed God to use me in ways I would never have dreamed of. During the latter years of my father's life he found his way back to the cross, and I know that someday I will see my father in Heaven. But the damage was done, and God's hedge was removed. He lost his marriage, his children and the abundant life that is found only in Christ and not in the occult.

I will tell you what happened to Intercession City. It happened to Jerusalem when the people were taken into captivity by the Babylonians and Jerusalem

became desolate and a heap of ruins. Osie England's ministry at Intercession
City was pulling down the strongholds of the devil. Intercession City was
crying out for worldwide revival and sending missionaries all over the world.
The kingdom of darkness was suffering much harm and the devil decided
to move against this city. His methods have not changed, and he uses his
age-old evil tactics. When my dad returned to Intercession City after the
war things were much different. Many of the people he knew had moved
away and things were not the same after the war. Let this be a lesson not to
ever remove yourself from other Christians and become isolated. He had no
transportation except a scooter. He worked constantly (mostly out of town)
and did not have time to assemble himself with the believers. When he was
not working out of town he was trying to build the log cabin. Like a piece
of hot charcoal when you remove it from the pile and isolate it, the fire goes
out. Then the enemy will entice you to take a substitute. My dad began to
entertain the occult and sought out palm readers and sorcery. He got into
voodoo and other forms of witchcraft until it destroyed his family. When he
lived in California he lived with a lady that was a palm reader. About the same
time that demons were working on my father, seeds of discord were planted
in Intercession City among Osie England's Christian workers and associates.
Teachers wanted more pay that Osie was not able to give them. There was
jealousy and trials over petty doctrines and externals, such as the wearing
of jewelry. The people became self-righteous. Because of the discord, Osie
England felt pressured to leave Intercession City in 1947, and made prepa-
ration to move her ministry to Sanford, Florida. After the school year ended
in 1948, it was the beginning of the exodus to Sanford, FL. Intercession City
would never be the same after that. When Miss. Osie departed Intercession
City, the Holy Spirit left with her. The Glory of God departed and as the
way of Jerusalem during the captivity so went Intercession City. Instead of
the best city to live in the State of Florida, it became the poorest just like
Jerusalem had become after the destruction of the city and their captivity

in Babylon. Intercession City became a byword like Jerusalem had become and the poorest of the poor reside there. During one of our prayer calls, praying over Intercession City, the Lord revealed that witches surrounded Intercession City with their chants and curses. Now we know as with Balaam and Balak in Numbers 22-24 that the enemy cannot touch you with curses as long as you walk in righteousness. But you can bring a curse upon yourself if you sin and turn away from God. Satan enticed the people of Intercession City to become self-righteous and conduct trials on one another over petty doctrines, dress, wearing of jewelry, etc. Instead of being content with their wages they complained and rose up against Osie England. They took on a religious spirit as with the Pharisees during Jesus day. It was said by one of our intercessor friends that religion crawled in bed with Jezebel and produced Ichabod—"The glory of God departed from Intercession City."

There were two men of prominence in Intercession that rose up against Osie England. The most prominent and vocal of the two was a powerful evangelist, Rev. C. L. Wireman, known as "Bulldog Charlie." Bulldog Charlie Wireman (Born 1890) was a converted Kentucky mountain outlaw said to be the "baddest" man in Kentucky during the early 1900s. Bulldog Charlie from his early teenage years was a confirmed drunkard and always carried a .45 caliber revolver with many notches in the handle denoting the number of men he had killed. He also carried a double action, improved Smith & Wesson in his pocket. The people of the town were afraid of him and avoided him. He would kill you at the drop of a hat. Bulldog Charlie was having an evil influence over the youth of the town. He was destroying homes and the lives of young people who in their twisted way of thinking looked up to Bull Dog Charlie as some sort of a hero and wanted to be like him.

A traveling evangelist came into town with a conviction to reach the youth. A saintly woman shared with the evangelist about Bulldog Charlie and the plight of the youth. They entered into a covenant of prayer along with others in the town to fast and pray until God either saves this young wicked man or move him out of town. When Bulldog Charlie heard that the evangelist was coming into town he vowed not to kill the preacher but would beat him and run him out of town. When the Methodist minister visited the town never having met Bulldog Charlie in person, he grabs his hand and says, "I am holding a revival in the Methodist Church. I don't believe I have noticed you in the revival. Won't you come and be with us?" He was caught off guard that a minister would walk up to him and invite him to a church service and found himself walking to the house of God. Bulldog Charlie was gloriously saved and transformed when the Evangelist gave the altar call. The fastings and prayers of the town had worked, and the man with the most notches on his gun became a new creation accepting the call of God on his life as an Evangelist. Bulldog Charlie was determined to serve God with as much fervor and zeal in winning the lost as he did in the world serving the devil and leading young people down the pathway of sin and destruction.

Bulldog Charlie held many tent revival services throughout Kentucky, Ohio and other places. It was perhaps in southern Ohio where he met Osie England during her camp meetings in the early part of the twentieth century. Bulldog Charlie moved to Intercession City and helped with the evangelism of the local area of Intercession City, Kissimmee, St. Cloud, Orlando and elsewhere and became known as the Dean of Evangelism with his church organization.

The division that occurred between Bulldog Charlie and Osie England was a difference in doctrine over when a person received the Holy Spirit. Bishop Osie England believed one received the Hold Spirit when they were born again or saved. Evangelist Bulldog Charlie believed one did not receive the Holy Spirit until they received the "Second Blessing" called "Sanitification." Bulldog Charlie split the church and took many of Osie's members to form the Wesleyan Methodist Church just two blocks down the street. This was very hurtful to Osie because she had a heart for everyone and always sought unity in the body of Christ. After Osie England left for Sanford, Florida during 1947-1948 school year the surviving members of H.C. Morrison Church, which was an independent church under Osie England's Household of Faith, voted to come under the Pilgrim Holiness Church denomination and was renamed Pilgrim Holiness. Later Bulldog Charlie repented for splitting the church and apologized to its members. It is not known whether or not Bulldog Charlie apologized directly to Osie England but the damage was done and the enemy succeeded is bringing division into the community. Later there was a second division. In 1968 the Wesleyan Methodist and Pilgrim Holiness denominations agreed to merge. When it came time for the Wesleyan Holiness Church (formed by Bulldog Charlie) in Intercession City to merge with the Pilgrim Holiness Church (formed by Osie England) in Intercession City, the current pastor at that time refused to merge and took his members to another location in Intercession City to form a separate church now known as the Lighthouse Baptist Church. Later the pastor felt he also was wrong in what he had done and expressed regret over his actions. He rebelled against the Wesleyan Methodist Church and they disciplined him by removing his license.

The other man of prominence who came against Osie England was Dr. Aaron Jacob (A. J.) Smith (1887-1960). He was the first president of Intercession City Bible College during the period before Osie England's departure (1942-1946) and later returned to serve as President under the new name of the College (Southern Wesleyan Bible College) from 1950 to 1952. Dr. A.J. Smith was also the President of Central Florida Bible School and College (now John Wesley College) and the first American to lead an organized expedition (Oriental Archeology Expedition) in search of Noah's Ark. Smith published a booklet about the expedition entitled *On the Mountains of Ararat in Quest of Noah's Ark*. Dr. Smith also is the author of several other books.

According to the story given me by the late historian T. J. Lavigne, there was a division over teacher's pay and Dr. A.J. Smith led the charge. Osie England was not able to give them the raises sought and there was bad feelings between the College and Osie England's organization. One has stated that after World War II there was a period of inflation which prompted the need for higher wages. Whether or not there was justification over wage increase, there was absolutely no justification for division. The late historian also shared with me that Osie England was put on ecclesiastical trial over differences in doctrine and that A. J. Smith was a part of this. Ironically, according to T.J. Lavigne, Mr. A. J. Smith was later put on ecclesiastical trial himself in regard to some of his writings.

If there is a lesson to learn in all of this is that we must never become divided. One of the most destructive tools Satan has in his toolbox is to cause division in the family, in the Church, on the job, and in the government. While in Point Pleasant, West Virginia where Osie England first started her ministry we ran across an article in Osie England's *Defender of the Faith* publication titled "Let Us Have Unity" published in 1923:

There is a certain town in the state of Ohio that has a population of 1,000. This same little town had four churches representing four different denominations. The people were greatly burdened in supporting or rather trying to support them. Some of their ministers were compelled to take up outside work to help earn a living. One of the pastors at one time suggested a union church, but the time was not yet ripe for that, and so nothing was done until the time came that all of the churches were without a preacher, except one. It was then that the people decided that they had too many churches for so small a town, so some of the trustees and leading members got together and considered a plan for uniting them.

The plan seemed a sensible one, and, strange to say, in the face of so much division these days, the majority of the people agreed to it and they were united into one. Now they have succeeded in making ONE large prosperous church grow where FOUR small non-prosperous ones grew before. They have chosen for their motto: **"In essentials, unity; In non-essentials, liberty; In diversities, charity; In all things! Christ first."**

No, none of these were holiness churches, it is true, but is not the ideal a good one for holiness folks to consider? Why so many denominations, so many divisions when there is only one Lord and one FAITH? (Eph. 4:5;. Why so many branches and only one VINE? (St. Jno. 15:5.) Why so many by-paths when there is only one WAY? Jesus said, "I am the way." (St. Jno. 14:6.) Why so much difficulty in finding the way when God has given us such a perfect Guide Book, and it has been so plainly marked but by those who have gone before?

Why worry about how we shall dress or talk or conduct ourselves to best please our Master when full directions are given us in the Word? Truly it is a "lamp unto our feet, a light unto our path" if we will but open our eyes and read. (See Ps. 119:105; 1 Tim. 2:9-10; 1 Pet. 3:1-4; Ps. 34:13;2 Pet. 3:11; also 1 Jno. 2:6, as examples of these simple directions.)

Let us, therefore, hold to the things that make for unity, pass by those that tend toward division, stick to the old paths and if we must be contentious, earnestly contend for the faith that was once delivered unto the saints.

Today many of the houses in Intercession City lie in ruin after "70 years of Captivity." This was once the most beautiful and prosperous city in Florida until its fall in1947, when Osie England was pressured to leave due to division, strife, and in-fighting. *Can the dead bones live again? God said He would breath on this City and they will come alive.*

Today many of the houses in Intercession City lie in ruin after "70 years of Captivity." This was once the most beautiful and prosperous city in Florida until its fall in1947, when Osie England was pressured to leave due to division, strife, and in-fighting. Can the dead bones live again? God said He would breath on this City and they will come alive.

5

OSIE ENGLAND AFTER HER DEPARTURE

After the split in 1947, due to division, jealously, infighting and issues over teachers' pay, Bishop Osie England left Intercession City, not because she wanted to but because she refused to compromise and submit to the pressure and ultimatums that some were putting on her. She left with Mr. Maddy, some of her staff and teachers and about half of the Bible School students and some residents. Some made their exodus after the end of the school year in 1948. They re-located in Sanford, Florida just 50 miles northwest of Intercession City on the Naval Air Station with a 99-year lease. Sanford Naval Air Station was commissioned on November 3, 1942, during World War II. The training base covered 3,000 acres of land and buildings with four runways. Peak wartime complements during 1943–1945 reached approximately 360 officers and 1400 enlisted men. After the War the Navy base was decommissioned in 1946, and the property leased out for commercial use under 99-year leases. In 1947, Osie England leased a portion of the Sanford Naval Air Station with a 99-year lease. This was a perfect place and opportunity to relocate her ministry and school. There she resumed the 100-Day Revival Meetings (3 services a day) and the Bible School and called the place Fellowship Front. A postcard mentions the Revival Meetings. This post card is about the 100-Day Revival Meetings—3 services a day at the Naval Air Station that they were leasing.

Dear Frannie & Charlie, -1-49

We are staying here at this Christian place called Fellowship Front, for a week, met some relatives of Weavers who are also here, have service's morning noon & night. Charlie says too much Religion. I enjoy, if all goes well, we will stop to see you on our way home about the last week in March,

Love to both, Rose & Charlie

Unfortunately, the 99-year lease arrangement was short lived. The base was recommissioned as Naval Auxiliary Air Station Sanford (NAAS Sanford) in 1950 in response to both the Korean War and the Cold War and subsequently re-designated as a full naval air station and renamed NAS Sanford. The Korean War and Cold War began in 1950 and the U.S. Fellowship Front had only been in existence in Sanford for three years, and now Osie is forced to move her school and ministry to another location.

Fellowship Front. After Osie England left Intercession City she leased facilities at the Naval Air Station in Sanford, Florida. She continued the 100-Day Revival Meetings – 3 Services a day

In 1951, after researching the area for a suitable location, Mr. Maddy purchased the Ormond Beach Hotel and The Casements across the street where John D. Rockefeller spent his winters and died in his bedroom in May 1937. Ormond Beach, Florida was less than 50 miles from their previous location in Sanford. For a second time Bishop Osie England is forced to re-locate her ministry and school. The Fellowship Center is established at the Ormond Beach Hotel. Across the street the Casements serves as the location for the school and also as a religious retirement facility where the elderly can purchase lifetime rooms or an apartment at a cost of $1,500 and upward.

The Hotel Ormond was the skyline signature of Ormond Beach for more than 100 years. It was built in 1887 by John Anderson and Joseph Price and opened January 1, 1888. Two years later Henry Flagler bought the hotel and made it into one of the best-known hotels in the world, a playground for the rich and famous of the time. Over the next 15 years Flagler added three new wings, expanding the number of rooms from 75 to 400, added elevators and a saltwater swimming pool, and built a railroad bridge from the mainland to the doors of the hotel. At the time it was the largest wooden structure in the United States and included 11 miles of corridors and breezeways. The hotel was located on 80 acres stretching from the Halifax River to the Atlantic Ocean. One of the hotel's most famous guests was Flagler's partner in the Standard oil Company, John D. Rockefeller, who spent several winters in the hotel before buying The Casements across the street in 1918. Other prominent guests included The Prince of Wales, Will Rogers, Henry Ford, Harvey Firestone, Thomas Edison, President Warren Harding, Harriet Beecher Stowe, George and Babe Zaharias, John Phillip Sousa, the Astors and Vanderbilts, and Al Capone. In 1923, Ed Sullivan became the golf secretary after he lost his newspaper job in Miami.

When John D. Rockefeller died in 1937, the period of elite patronage began a steady decline. A succession of new owners took over. In 1949 Robert Woodward bought the hotel from Flagler's Florida East Coast Hotel Company. In 1951 C.A. Maddy purchased the hotel to sell lifetime contracts to the elderly and to provide a place for Osie's school and ministry. Two years later in 1953 Mr. C. A. Maddy, Osie's most gifted businessman and partner in ministry, dies from pneumonia. After that things started to go downhill for Osie. Osie England's Ormond Beach location went bankrupt.

The government broke Osie England's 99-Year lease in Sanford due to the Korean and Cold Wars. Her next move was to the Grand Hotel Ormond and the Casements across the street

The hotel was sold in a bankruptcy auction in 1955, and Osie England returns to Point Pleasant, West Virginia where she first started her ministry. She resumed her ministry there and finished well with her assistant, Kathleen Sargent Slenker. Arabella and I had the opportunity to interview Kathleen and learn the rest of the story of Osie before the departure of this great woman of faith and intercessor unto her everlasting reward in Heaven.

I am sure at Point Pleasant, West Virginia Osie England reflected back on the tremendous success God had given her in Intercession City and the disappointing ending at Ormond Beach. While Arabella was praying one evening on the floor (this was the same time the Lord told Arabella to do the 100-day prayer revival), she inquired of the Lord as to what caused Osie England to leave Intercession City. What was it that she did not do? The Lord answered and said: "She grew weary in well doing, and that is what caused her to leave." Bishop Osie England was on the brink of praying in a worldwide revival, but the enemy ran her out. Her work was not finished in Intercession City. Now it is time to complete the work that Osie started in Intercession City. Now is the time for the intercessors across Florida to take ownership of God's city and pray in the last day harvest.

Point Pleasant, West Virginia

Point Pleasant, West Virginia is where Bishop Osie England started her ministry (West Virginia Training Center and the Mountain State Orphanage). We had the opportunity of visiting England Memorial in February 2018. Bishop Osie England's activities included: Bible Training School, Orphanage, Homes for the elderly, Camp meetings, Tabernacles for Camp Meetings, Home and Foreign Missions training center, and Defender of the Faith magazine.

Kathleen Sargent Slenker

Osie England's Assistant in Point Pleasant, WV after leaving Ormond Beach, Florida. Kathleen came to Point Pleasant as an orphan and became Osie's most trusted and close associate. We had the pleasure of interviewing Ms. Kathleen Slenker in February 2018. Kathleen showed us all of Osie England's historical documents, newspaper clippings, old photos, diaries, etc. After Osie England was called home in 1957 Kathleen became her successor.

From *The Book of Osie or The Life of Bishop Osie England*:

"Rev. Kathleen Sargent, ordained minister, evangelist, pastor, and present superintendent of the West Virginia Training School also came under the influence of this godly leader (Osie England). The deathbed request to Miss Sargent was, 'Will you stay with the School?' An affirmative answer 'As long as the Lord leads,' brought a smile upon the dying face of the one who was faithful until death. Miss Sargent has assumed many of the tasks and burdens that come with operating a Bible School. In a variety of ways it appears that Miss England's mantle of wisdom, counseling of youth, generosity, and tenderheartedness fell upon this able superintendent of West Virginia Training School.

6

PROCLAMATION CAN THESE DEAD BONES LIVE AGAIN?

After Osie England was pressured to leave Intercession City in 1947, the Intercession City Bible College (ICBC) continued. (Osie England had sold the facilities to the college upon her departure.) Dr. A. J. Smith, its first President (1942-1946) in which there was division with Miss. Osie, left and Charles W. Rice became President from 1946-1948. The name of the college was changed to Southern Wesleyan Bible College. Mr. Hayes succeeded Charles W. Rice in 1949. The following year Dr. A. J. Smith returned as President of Southern Wesleyan Bible College and served from 1950-1952. The final President was Harry E. Jessop who was President from 1952-1956. A decade after Osie's departure the College failed, and Intercession City continued its decline both spiritually and physically. The once bustling pristine city fell in decay. No longer was it a Christian community (God's city of 24-hour prayer) having no alcohol, tobacco, gambling, prostitution, or other vices but a dumping place where sin abounded (drug addition, alcoholism, etc.) Prisoners who served their time and had no family were released into Intercession City. Businesses left and growth stagnated. The population dynamics changed and the medium income for Intercession City became the lowest in the State of Florida. Do not get me wrong. Yes, there are churches and prayer in Intercession City and many good works are being done here for the Kingdom of God. But compared to yesterday it is like day and night. The church Osie England established is still in existence and other churches of different denominations have sprung up. Osie England's church was first called The Large House of Prayer and named Morrison Memorial Church. A second church was established called Pilgrim Holiness. In 1968 The Wesleyan Methodist (Morrison Memorial) and the Pilgrim Holiness merged to form the Wesleyan Church, now named Community Wesleyan Church currently pastored by Rev. Don White. The outer structure is basically the same as it was in Osie England's day. It was such an honor for Arabella and I to be married at the front of the church near the pulpit area where Bishop Osie England preached. Arabella and I also had the privilege of being ordained at this very spot by Arabella's spiritual mother, Rev. Noel Simone, who carries the mantle of Norvel Hayes, who carried the mantle of Lester Sumrall, who carried the mantle of Smith Wigglesworth.

We are honored to take the mantle and believe God for signs, wonders and miracles in the last days before His coming so that millions of souls can be brought into the Kingdom of God.

Ezekiel 37 talks about the valley of dead bones. Most people having driven through Intercession City see an impoverished area with no prospect of future growth or prosperity. They view Intercession City as Ezekiel did when he saw the valley of dead parched bones. God said to him: "Son of man, can these bones live." God is asking us that same question today in regard to Intercession City: "Can this city live again?" I say yes: "INTERCESSION CITY SHALL LIVE AGAIN."

In recent years the ground has been prepared for the return of God's glory to His city. A number of Godly men and women walked the streets praying, worshipping and declaring the Word over Intercession City. Several had deep feelings for Intercession City that there was something prophetic about this place—God wanted to do something special here. Even visitors sensed it. An artist by the name of June Taylor painted a vision of what is coming to Intercession City—A Whirlwind of Glory and Holiness! During the 24-hour prayer convergence October 6-7, 2017, at the Community Wesleyan Church one of the intercessors, Karen Ledbetter, not having seen the June Taylor painting, had the same vision and painted a whirlwind of God's Glory on Intercession City similar to the one June Taylor painted.

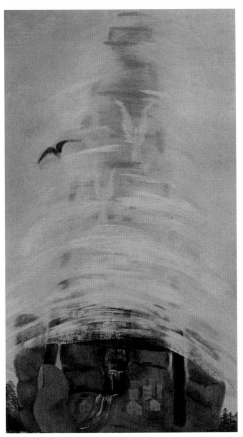 

June Taylor's Painting   *Karen Ledbetter's Painting*

In March of 2014 many of the pastors and ministry leaders of Intercession City joined together to seek God at the Community Wesleyan Church to be personally transformed and set apart for His glory, and they began to meet one night weekly at the Wesleyan Church to pray as priest of the Most High God seeking Him to manifest His glory in the city, the state and the nation—taking up the shovel to re-dig the old wells and to dig new wells of revival. During one of the prayer meetings, T J Lavigne, the late historian of Intercession City was taken up in the Spirit. The following is his account:

The Lord showed me how He views Intercession city. T J Lavigne: **Ezekiel 37:1 The Lord took hold of me, and I was carried away by the Spirit of the Lord to a valley filled with bones.** *NLT Even as Ezekiel was carried away by the Spirit of the Lord, I was carried away in the Spirit as I sat praying with my back to the window inside the Large House of Prayer (LHOP) in Intercession City, Florida. I had the sensation of travelling backwards into outer space, into the 1st heaven (outer space), where I came to a stop and looked down and was looking the crystal dome over Intercession City in the fall of 2015.*

God's Crystal Dome over Intercession City: Intercession City's Crystal Dome is a protective dome that will shield the people of Intercession City from God's enemies in behalf of his people. When Revival hits Intercession City, this Dome will be installed by God. Ephesians 6:12 For we wrestle not against flesh and blood, but against principalities, against powers, against the rulers of the darkness of this world, against spiritual wickedness in high places. My original vision as I was translated into the 1st heaven and seeing a crystal like, shimmering, dome, over Intercession City, as I prayed with the group in the Wesleyan Church. The dome below is similar to the one I saw, even though this one is over a large city. In the spring of July 2016, I realized that there is a correlation of the Chrystal Dome I saw over Intercession City and the Iron Dome over Israel. Israel's Iron Dome was inspired by God but built by man. Intercession City's Crystal Dome is being put in place per order and by the Lord God.

Hallelujah. This was not a spiritual vision, open vision or trance type vision. This is an experience where my spirit/soul came out of my body and I travelled into space over Intercession City, and when I stopped travelling, I hung there looking down at the beautiful sparkling dome over the community. It was already night time and I could see the I.C. streets beneath the dome and there were hundreds of shining lights, like bright LED twinkling lights on all the streets. I hung in space for a short time and then began my back through the window and into my chair. I then told those who were praying what had just happened to me. I was stunned by this experience because nothing like this had ever happened to me.

TJ Lavigne: God's Crystal Dome over Intercession City (This is similar to what I saw)

Having discovered my roots in Intercession City through my Dad's photo album during the summer of 2016; and, having linked my father's photos as one of the pioneers with Osie England of Intercession City through Ted Lavigne's website, I became connected with T J Lavigne and he invited me to speak on Osie England Day on April 7, 2017. (Osie was celebrated on her birthday each year on April 7th at the park in Intercession City). The Lord had spoken to me that He would use me as an apostle to rebuild Intercession

City and gave me a proclamation to speak over the city and also to pray forgiveness for the sins of our fathers and forefathers. The following is my proclamation of life over Intercession City. "The dead bones shall live again" Ezekiel 37.

Proclamation

Today, on the 7th day of April, the 17th year of a new millennial, exactly 70 years ago when the devil almost destroyed me and stole my family and ran Miss Osie and other men and women of God out of town through splits and division, marks 70 years of captivity and poverty. I declare this day, Osie England Day, the 5777th year of the Jewish calendar, as the beginning of a new day for this city. The former glory of this city is about to return. Once again it will be a sparkling shinning city with the reflection of the Glory of God. Once again people will gather to this city from not only the United States but from all over the world to study God's word and be sent out into the fivefold ministries (apostles, prophets, evangelist, pastors, and teachers.) There will be many millennials trained in this city to change the world before the return of our Savior. Once again, the prayer chapel will be rebuilt and there will be prayers going up to Heaven all day and all night. But this time the devil will not be able to destroy this town like he did before. No devil in hell or out of hell will be able to defeat you. God himself will place a shield over us. It will be a protective dome He will hide us in the cleft of the rock and cover us with His hand. Isaiah 61:4. And they shall build the wastes of old, they shall raise up the former desolations, and they shall repair the waste cities, the desolations of many generations. There will be an open heaven to accomplish this. A huge portal from the heavenlies to Intercession City. It will be like Jacob's dream of the ladder from heaven with angels descending and ascending. No longer will Intercession City be a dumping ground but a city of attraction. A city having everlasting joy that surpasses the thrill of Disney's Magic Kingdom.

But we must first repent as Nehemiah did not only for his sins but those of his father. Nehemiah 1:3 records the report that was given to Nehemiah after Jerusalem was surveyed: They said to me, "Those who survived the exile and are back in the province are in great trouble and disgrace. The wall of Jerusalem is broken down, and its gates have been burned with fire." When I heard these things, I sat down and wept. For some days I mourned and fasted and prayed before the God of heaven. Then I said: "Lord, the God of heaven, the great and awesome God, who keeps his covenant of love with those who love him and keep his commandments, let your ear be attentive and your eyes open to hear the prayer your servant is praying before you day and night for your servants, the people of Israel. I confess the sins we Israelites, including myself and my father's family, have committed against you. We have acted very wickedly toward you. We have not obeyed the commands, decrees and laws you gave your servant Moses."

Our Prayer of Confession for Intercession City

"Oh Lord, our God. Our Heavenly Father—The great and mighty God who loves us with an everlasting love and judges the world in righteousness. Who has not forsaken us, but we have forsaken you Lord? Forgive my sins and the sins of my father that were committed here 70 years ago in this your city of prayer. Also, forgive those who touched your anointed and did your servants harm. Father, do not hold this sin against this city but cover it over with your blood and separate all of the past and present sins of Intercession City as far as the east is from the west. May this city once again be your dwelling place, and may your glory shine forth again to change the world. In the precious name of our Savior, Jesus Christ."

What are we waiting on? For more souls to be damned to hell. For missed opportunities to train millennials into the fivefold ministries to go forth from this city with power and anointing to change the world for Christ before His return.

*Now is the time to build. Now is our finest hour. Ezra 3:1 The people assembled as one man in Jerusalem. Let's build together. Let's not be divided ever again. The people had a mind to work. Let's get to work. You may be waiting for the resources to come before moving out in faith. I say move in faith and God will provide the resources as you go just as in the days of Ezra and Nehemiah—As they went provisions were ordered by Cyrus to rebuild Jerusalem and the Temple. **Can the dead bones and dead hearts live again? God said He would breath on this city and they will come alive.***

Three months later on July 5, 2017, Dr. Negiel BigPond of the First Nation was led of God to come to the Community Wesleyan Church in Intercession City. He usually ministers in larger cities, but God brought him here to pray and break the curses of the past because of the injustices, cruelty pain and sufferings by the First Nation People in Florida. Negiel BigPond shed a tear and forgave the injustices that took place here among the First Nation People.

Not long afterwards the worship leader, Kent Henry, was led of the Lord to come to the Wesleyan Church in Intercession City on Sunday, July 16, 2017, for a 2 pm service. There were about 30 in attendance. Kent Henry played the piano and led in Worship. The glory of God fell in the Wesleyan Church once again. They worshipped, interceded, prophesied, anointed the walls, doors, posts, altar rails and windows with oil. Kent instructed the group to do a Jericho March around the sanctuary marching around the sanctuary seven (7) times.

The following October 2017, through Divine Providence God brought Arabella Robinson to Intercession City to pray over the region. God had mandated that she hold 24-hour prayer convergences throughout the State of Florida. Arabella created Rise-Up ONE UNITED VOICE to support intercessors throughout Florida and elsewhere. Her mission is: "No Intercessor down,

No Intercessor alone, No Intercessor left behind." She carries "UNITY" John 17 across Florida. While looking for a place to hold her October 6-7 Convergence God led one of the Intercessors traveling from Key Largo to Satellite Beach, Florida to make an exit off of Interstate 4 that took her to Intercession City. Her first comment was: "Where are the intercessors." After Googling and reading about Osie and the rich history from T J Lavigne's website she immediately contacted Arabella. Arabella was so excited to hear about Osie England and Intercession City. What better place to have a 24-hour intercessory prayer convergence than in Intercession City. She contacted the local pastor and secured arrangements at the Wesleyan Church to hold the convergence during the Feast of Tabernacles on October 6-7, 2017. It was called Feast of Tabernacles—Intercessors Unity Pilgrimage. This convergence in Intercession City brought Arabella and I together.

The first 24-hour prayer convergence in Intercession City held during the Feast of Tabernacles October 6-7, 2017.

Prior to the Convergence Arabella held a Pre-Convergence meeting in Intercession City on Saturday September 23rd, 2017. What was so powerful at the Pre-Convergence meeting was a season of remorse and repentance for the sins of the intercessors, their parents, and the past sins of Intercession City.

Wesley reads the Intercessor's Confession and repents for his sins, those of his father, and the sins of the people of Intercession City. Must first have repentance and redemption, and then the re-building of God's altars can be established.

A Land Redemption Service was held in front of the Community Wesleyan Church in Intercession City on September 22, 2017, by Marsha McArthur. We anointed the Land (Intercession City), dropped the plumb line, had communion, and prayed for the healing of the Land in Intercession City. We all signed the deed which stated: "This land is now and shall remain free from any ungodly spiritual encumbrances or liens of the kind from this day thru eternity. Because of the saving grace of the shed blood of Jesus Christ. This deed is hereby freely transferred to Jehovah God, The Creator of Heaven and Earth, as a clear title. It was during this time of the pre-convergence that Arabella and I married. We were married September 25, 2017, just after the pre-convergence.

7

UNITY MARRIES THE LAND

When the Father brought Wesley and Arabella together through Divine Providence it was to bring "Unity to the Land". Wesley represents the "LAND" in the heart of Florida: Orlando area and Intercession City. Intercession City is the spiritual capitol of Florida and measurably the very center of Florida (north, south, east and west). Wesley's father (Lawrence Weaver) was a pioneer family that helped build Intercession City (the City of Prayer) and on his mother's side, Aaron Jernigan, a distant cousin of Wesley, was the first settler of Orlando, brought in the first 700 cattle, and obtained 1,200 acres of land near Fort Gatlin. The City was first named "Jernigan." As a representative of the LAND Wesley carried Isaiah 62 of God being reconciled to the land and no longer termed forsaken or desolate but called Beulah (married) and Hephzibah (My delight is in her). Arabella took Unity (John 17) throughout Florida, driving the entire coastline and panhandle of Florida, anointing the beaches and ground, and proclaiming unity and the perfect will of the Father through the State. The following was written by Wesley just prior to their marriage on September 25, 2017. The marriage was celebrated at the Community Wesleyan Church at the altar where Miss. Osie England stood and preached many times. Wesley and Arabella were later ordained here by her spiritual mother, Rev. Simone Noel of God's Embassies International—a part of Norvel Hayes ministries for many years.

WHEN UNITY MARRIES THE LAND
By Wesley Weaver

UNITY: Arabella A. Robinson (John 17)
LAND: Wesley J. Weaver (Isaiah 62)
United in Matrimony: September 25, 2017

When Unity marries the Land no longer does unrighteousness and sin prevail, but righteousness shall once again return to this place and those around you shall see your righteousness.

When Unity marries the Land, you shall no longer be termed Forsaken, nor shall your land any more be termed Desolate. For the Glory of God shall return and the kings of the earth shall see your glory.

When Unity marries the Land mourning and sorrow shall flee away. They will come and shout for joy on the heights of Zion; they will rejoice in the bounty of the Lord— the grain, the new wine and the olive oil, the young of the flocks and herds. They will be like a well-watered garden, and they will sorrow no more. Then young women will dance and be glad, young men and old as well. I will turn their mourning into gladness; I will give them comfort and joy instead of sorrow. Jeremiah 31:12-13

When Unity marries the Land once again shall streams of water spring up from the Wells of Salvation to flow freely throughout a dry and thirsty Land. Her salvation shall be a lamp that burns like a torch. The Holy Fire that was once extinguished shall burn again and this place shall be like a city set on a hill which cannot be hid.

When Unity marries the Land no longer shall this Land be called Ichabod—
The Glory of God has departed—but shall be called The City of Zion, the
new Jerusalem of Florida, Hephzibah—My delight is in her—and Beulah
meaning " Married"—A Land flowing with milk and honey.

When Unity marries the Land no longer shall the Land be uninhabited as
in Jeremiah 9:11 when God said, "I will make Jerusalem a heap of ruins, a
haunt of jackals; and I will lay waste the towns of Judah so no one can live
there." But this Land shall be sought out and once again inhabited and the
sound of music, singing and dance shall return to the streets of this city.

When Unity marries the Land no longer shall the Land be unfruitful but the
seed God has planted in the Land and in the lives of Wesley and Arabella
shall yield abundant fruit that remains, producing an abundant harvest not
only in this city but in Florida, the Nation, and the Uttermost parts of the
world—a revival of worldwide proportion Osie England so longed for.

When Unity marries the Land, it shall no longer be a place of gloom and sad-
ness but rejoicing—a city filled with joy and gladness. For the Lord delights
in you when Unity marries the Land. For as a young man marries a virgin
and rejoices over her, so shall your God rejoice over you.

"Unity Marries the Land" September 25, 2017

Ordination Ceremony by Rev. Simone Noel February 4, 2018

8

REBIRTHING OF INTERCESSION CITY

The Feast of Tabernacle Convergence in Intercession City on October 6-7, 2017, was the conception and the beginning of the rebirthing of Intercession City. The following July 2018, the Lord had directed Arabella to have a Koinonia gathering of seasoned intercessors that functioned in their respective assignments—each to teach from their knowledge and experience to the other intercessors. It was also an opportunity for fellowship and getting to know intercessors from around the State of Florida and elsewhere. It was held at the Intercession City Church of God. When Arabella set the date of July 6-7, 2018, she was not aware that it was exactly nine months after the conception date (Our very first meeting—Feast of Tabernacle October 6-7th) in Intercession City, just after Arabella and I were married. This would be the rebirthing of Intercession City. The dead bones spoken of in Ezekiel 37 will come alive again.

The Year of the Push and Open Door

Around May of 2018, while in prayer for the intercessors Arabella had a vision of two Intercessors in front of two large heavy wooden double doors. One intercessor was on the right side and the other on the left. They were holding a large battering ram, ramming and pushing it against the locked doors. As the intercessors began pushing on the doors Arabella heard a voice saying: "Push, Push!" As they began ramming the huge doors with this big square battering ram that looked like a boulder, the Father showed Arabella thousands and thousands of Intercessors standing behind the two Intercessors. There were so many she could only see the top of their heads. As they began to push in rhythmic unity the door began to crack open. Afterwards Arabella shared on Rise-Up ONE UNITED VOICE Facebook live her vision encouraging the Intercessors to keep pushing. The following week the Lord woke Arabella up from a nap with a dream/vision of Jenny Weaver (Anointed Worshiper). Jenny was speaking to Arabella saying: "Don't stop pushing, keep pushing, keep pushing! This is the year of the push! This is the year of the push!" Arabella inquired of the Lord: What is meant by: "This is the year of the push?" "Isn't this the year of the open door." Father spoke to Arabella and said, "Yes, this is the year of the open door, but it will take the prayers of the intercessors to push the door open".

In Chapter 9 "Intercession City Lives Again—Eight Gates to the City" on the graph you will see the "Hub" of Intercession City surrounded by Intercessors. There are Intercessors assigned to each of the eight walls and entrance ways (doors or gates). As mentioned above Intercessors will function in the passion God has called them—to pray the perfect will of the Father in their areas of passion or assignment. Some interceding for revival and souls, some for the government, some for education, some for the market place and economy, and some pro-life, etc.

Three weeks prior to returning back to Intercession City and hosting the Koinonia Intercessors Gathering, Father spoke to Arabella and said: "Go on Facebook live and release my voice every day until you enter the City." Then He said: "As you (release my voice) I will command, order, align and create into my Intercessors lives daily. On one of the Facebook live videos

Arabella began to feel this fullness and announced: "There is an Intercessor out there birthing." Then the Lord said: "Why can't that be you?" Arabella responded: "What am I birthing?" He began to show the timeline that there were nine months from the time you married Wesley on Sep 25th until the time of your arrival on June 25th to your new home near Intercession City. Also, the Koinonia Intercessors Gathering held July 5-7, 2018 was exactly nine months from the first Feast of Tabernacles Convergence held in Intercession City on Oct 6-7, 2017. At this Koinonia gathering many of the Intercessors began experiencing birthing pains in the Spirit for the rebirth of Intercession City (July 6, 2018). In fact, there were twin birthing believed to be God's "GRACE" and "MERCY" over Intercession City.

The Koinonia Gathering July 6-7, 2019

The Koinonia Gathering July 6-7, 2019

Rev. Simone Noel, One of our Speakers

Prayers of Unity Among our Leaders

Jenny Weaver

Scherilyn Phelps

Anointed Worship Leaders

Those participating in the Prayer Walk in Intercession City during the Koinonia Gathering

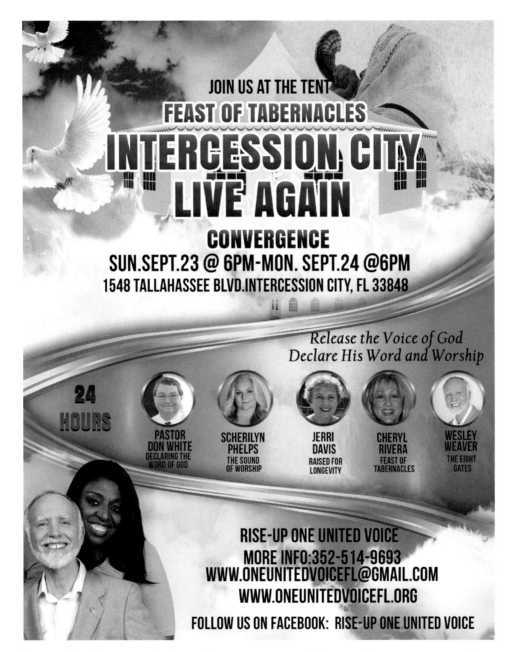

The Second 24-hour Feast of Tabernacle Convergence was held September 23-24, 2018, On the very spot where the 24-7 Prayer Cabin stood (The Music Emporium) on Old Tampa Highway, Intercession City.

During the prayer walk at the Koinonia Intercessors Gathering on Saturday, July 7th, 2018, we came to a location where one of the prayer cabins stood. The Lord spoke to Arabella: "This is where the next Convergence is to be. Put a tent up here." Arabella was unaware that this was the very place where Osie England's third prayer cabin stood (The Music Emporium). There was so much resistance in getting the permits, but approval came through just one day prior to the Convergence beginning September 23rd. This was the Second Annual 24-hour Prayer Convergence in Intercession City. We knew then that the synergy of the ages had begun. There was a powerful presence of God during the Feast of Tabernacle prayer gathering.

Before the tent was erected, we prayed and walked the perimeter of the lot where the prayer cabin stood, anointed the land, and drove a stake in the ground.

A 30 X 50-foot tent was erected near the intersection of Tallahassee Boulevard and Old Tampa Highway. The first night we had about 45 people in attendance.

9

INTERCESSION CITY LIVES AGAIN

The Plan Moving Forward

God gave Nehemiah a plan to rebuild Jerusalem. God has a plan for rebuilding Intercession City. To rebuild we must all work together in unity as a community. We must unite under a common cause to meet the needs of the community, raise it standards, and contend for souls. It is not a project just for one church, one ministry, one organization, or one man, but for the whole of the community. Nor is it a plan for the faint at heart or unbeliever. Nehemiah did not invite just a few chosen to rebuild. He utilized all the people within the city to build. The families worked together to rebuild and protect their section of the wall—with one hand they worked at construction and with the other held a weapon.

Intercessors Key to Praying the Perfect Will of the Father

During a Dutch Sheets meeting on December 1, 2017, in Satellite Beach, Florida Arabella was sitting in Kingdom Gate Church and God spoke to her about an Apostolic Center (Hub) as Dutch was preaching on it and gave identity to Rise-Up ONE UNITED VOICE Network (Unity Net-Sphere of Intercessors). Father spoke and said I've called Rise-Up to be like an Apostolic Center (Hub) where my Intercessors will function in their passion, I've called them to. Some government. Some passion will be education, other souls, and so on. But you will support all streams—an Apostolic Alignment of Intercessors supporting each other, having a relationship that I birth, that is unusual but much unity. There will be resistance as always to what I assign, and I do. But it is done and all that are supposed to be a part will—and others won't—but they are not My real Intercessors called in this hour and season.

As mentioned above Rise-Up ONE UNITED VOICE is likened to a hub. All Intercessors have been given an assignment to intercede the perfect will of the Father upon the earth. The Apostolic Hub (Rise-Up ONE UNITED VOICE) will have an Embassy for Intercessors to receive training and support to carry their assignment as they go forth in obedience. It shall go all around the world. Like a circle or sphere with lines (nets) going out all around the world. Their prayer shall go out not only for Intercession City,

Florida and the Nation but for the entire world. God gave Wesley "Unity Net-Sphere of Intercessors" which has been incorporated in Rise-Up ONE UNITED VOICE Network of Intercessors who have joined together for this purpose.

God's Vision for the City

After the Koinonia Intercessors Gathering July 5th through 7th, God gave Arabella and Wesley a plan. God showed Arabella seven needs of Intercession City. But after Arabella had written down the seven needs the Lord showed Arabella that there was one more and exclaimed: "No, there are eight needs." God's vision of the eight needs of Intercession City as follows:

1. **Prayer & Ministry Centers—Embassy for Intercessors.**
2. **Health and Drug Rehabilitation Services.**
3. **Social Services—Thrift Shop, Food Center, Refire Establishments.**
4. **Community Outreach—Evangelism, Revival**
5. **Government—City Incorporation/Municipality**
6. **Market Place—Economy**
7. **Rebuilding—New Housing**
8. **Learning, Teaching & Training Center -Education**

Immediately afterwards the Lord began to download the entire vision based on the eight needs of the City. The Lord showed Wesley an octagon of eight walls for Intercession City—each side (wall) of the octagon is represented by each of the needs. It dawned on us that the number eight was for "open doors" for the year 2018. Later that night the Lord prompted Wesley to look up the Gates of Jerusalem. Wesley said to himself, I hope there are eight gates because I could assign a gate for each of the eight walls of the octagon and the eight needs of the community. Wesley looked up the gates of the Old City of Jerusalem and found there were eight. He put together a graph (Hub) for Intercession City which depicts the vision for the city. Below is a graph (INTERCESSION CITY LIVES AGAIN—THE VISION FOR INTERCESSION CITY) with a written description explaining the different parts of the Hub. The Word states in Habakkuk 2:2 "Write the vision and make it plain on tablets." Wesley spent the entire night writing the vision of the Eight Gates of the City.

The Hub of Intercession City

Intercession City is likened to an eight sided "Hub" (octagon) representing "The Jerusalem of Florida." Each of the eight sides of the city (walls) has a gate named after the eight gates of the old City of Jerusalem (entrance ways for the restoration of Intercession City). The Year 2018 is the year of open doors. We are believing God to shut the gates of the enemy to Intercession City, establish His Altar, and open wide His Portal so that His plans and agenda for Intercession City be fulfilled. It is for His Glory and not that of man. We have prayed in the rebirth now is the time to restore the City for longevity. We are praying for an Embassy for Intercessors and 24-hour prayer cabins so that this City can Rise-Up and once again become a Spiritual Center not only for Florida, but for the Nation and the World which was God's original vision for Intercession City given to its founder, Osie England, for worldwide revival. This would include meeting the eight needs of Intercession City which includes the eight gates as depicted on the chart.

In the previous chapter it was revealed that the Year 2018 was the Year of the Push and Open Door. The Gates to Intercession City will be cracked open with incessant prayers by the Intercessors. As the Intercessors continue to pray earnestly over the eight needs of Intercession City we will see great breakthroughs. But, it must be a unified effort of prayer. The Bible tells us in Psalm 127:1 that unless the Lord builds the house, they labor in vain who build it. Intercession City was established through intercessory prayer and will be re-built with intercessory prayer. The Bible also states in Joshua 23:10 that one man shall chase a thousand. How much power is generated when a thousand intercessors pray as ONE? There will be exponential results when many intercessors are in agreement prayer—the eight gates of Intercession City will be blown off their hinges. The Lord showed Arabella thousands and thousands of Intercessors standing behind the two Intercessors in front of the door with the battering ram. There were so many she could only see the top of their heads. As they began to push in rhythmic unity the door began to crack open. The Intercessors will be the key to the revitalization of Intercession City.

On the graph you will see the "Hub" of Intercession City surrounded by Intercessors. There are Intercessors assigned to each of the eight walls and entrance ways (Gates). As mentioned above Intercessors will function in the passion God has called them—to pray the perfect will of the Father in their areas of passion or assignment. Some interceding for revival and souls, some for the government, some for education, some for the market place and economy, etc. The Intercessors may or may not participate directly in rebuilding Intercession City, but their prayers are vital to the rebirthing of the city. They are the ones with the battering ram that will crack open the eight entrances to the City during the year of the Open Door (2018) so that the eight needs of Intercession City come to fruition.

The Eight Gates (Entrance Doors) to Intercession City

Previously under "God's Vision for the City" I shared the vision God had given me as I was mediating on the eight needs of Intercession City. I described an octagon shaped city with eight walls, each wall representing one of the eight needs of Intercession City; and, the Lord speaking to me to look up the gates of the old city of Jerusalem. When I went online to search, I was elated to find exactly eight gates to the City of Jerusalem. I applied each of the eight gates (entrance ways) of the old city of Jerusalem to Intercession City Eight Gates—the Jerusalem of Florida.

A description of the eight gates of old Jerusalem can be found at the following link *The Gates of Jerusalem*: https://new.goisrael.com/article/252

The eight gates described in the link above are as follows starting on the south side of the old city Jerusalem moving counter-clockwise from south to west. (Corresponding as follows on the graph: Start at the bottom side of the octagon and move counter-clockwise)

1. **The Zion Gate**
2. **The Dung Gate**
3. **Gate of Mercy**
4. **Lion's Gate**
5. **Herod's Gate**
6. **Damascus Gate**
7. **The New Gate**
8. **The Jaffa Gate**

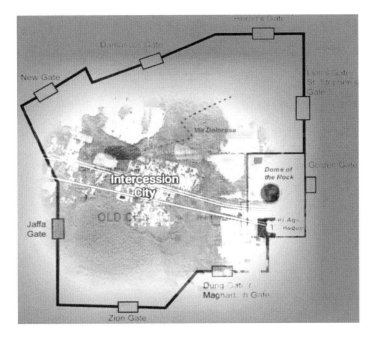

The Walls and Eight Gates of Jerusalem superimposed over Intercession City. As Jerusalem was centrally located in Israel and was its Spiritual Capitol, so is Intercession City: The Jerusalem of Florida and known in Osie England's day as The Religious capital of Florida – The very center and heart of Florida.

The Eight Needs of Intercession City
The Father's Plan, His Doors and His Agenda

Before you build there must be an assessment of the City to determine the needs of the people and the City itself. Before Nehemiah began rebuilding Jerusalem, he first surveyed the city and took an assessment. When we first arrived in Intercession, we surveyed the city and found there were many needs here. We must reach out first in love to the community and meet the spiritual and physical needs of the poor. The people will not respond on empty stomachs with little income. Some are already providing help to the community. We must expand this with not only feeding centers but with other services, such as, social, health, housing, elderly care, etc. The City itself must be assessed to raise its standards from a poor community to a thriving town with a revitalization program—establishing a city government, new businesses, housing projects, etc. But most importantly there must be a return of prayer centers and ministry outreach to satisfy the spiritual needs of the lost and hurting. Inside each of the walls of the city on the graph you will find the eight areas of needs listed in blue counter-clockwise, starting from the bottom of the octagon:

1. **THE ZION GATE—Isaiah 62:1-2**
   Prayer & Ministry Centers—Embassy for Intercessors.

   Holy Spirit directed The Zion Gate for the Prayer & Ministry Centers because Zion represents the heavenly City of Jerusalem and Mount Zion. Intercession City again shall become the City of Zion with 24-hour Prayer Cabins, Ministry Centers, and an Embassy for Intercessors.

   For Zion's sake I will not hold My peace,
   And for Jerusalem's sake I will not rest,
   Until her righteousness goes forth as brightness,

And her salvation as a lamp that burns.
The Gentiles shall see your righteousness,
And all kings your glory.
You shall be called by a new name,
Which the mouth of the Lord will name. Isaiah 62:1-2

2. **THE DUNG GATE—Isaiah 61:1-4**
   Health and Drug Rehabilitation Services.

The Dung Gate represents Health and Drug Rehab Services. Dung represent filth and we want to remove all the filth in Intercession City through the Dung Gate by establishing a health clinic for the poor, alcohol and drug abuse programs, etc. During the time of Osie England Intercession City was a pristine clean community. There was no alcohol, gambling, smoking, prostitution, or other vices allowed.

"The Spirit of the Lord God is upon Me,
Because the Lord has anointed Me
To preach good tidings to the poor;
He has sent Me to heal the brokenhearted,
To proclaim liberty to the captives,
And the opening of the prison to those who are bound;
To proclaim the acceptable year of the Lord,
And the day of vengeance of our God;
To comfort all who mourn,
To console those who mourn in Zion,
To give them beauty for ashes,
The oil of joy for mourning,
The garment of praise for the spirit of heaviness;
That they may be called trees of righteousness,

The planting of the Lord, that He may be glorified."And they shall rebuild the old ruins,
They shall raise up the former desolations,
And they shall repair the ruined cities,
The desolations of many generations. Isaiah 61:1-4

3. **GATE OF MERCY—Matthew 25:34-40: Matthew 6:31-34**
Social Services, Thrift Shop, Food Center, Refire establishments.

Jesus always shows compassion for the poor and needy. We must do the same. Therefore, the Gate of Mercy represents the need for social services, thrift shop, food center, care for the elderly, etc. in Intercession City. We are to show mercy to the poor. Matthew 5:7 states "Blessed are the merciful for they shall obtain mercy." Intercession City shall be a community that serves one another, supporting and caring for its neighbors. There shall be no lack as the Kingdom of God shall be demonstrated through the provision of attending to the needs of the people. "Pure and undefiled religion before God and the Father is this: To visit orphans and widows in their trouble . . . "James 1:27.

Then the King will say to those on His right hand, 'Come, you blessed of My Father, inherit the kingdom prepared for you from the foundation of the world: 35 for I was hungry and you gave Me food; I was thirsty and you gave Me drink; I was a stranger and you took Me in; 36 I was naked and you clothed Me; I was sick and you visited Me;I was in prison and you came to Me.' "Then the righteous will answer Him, aying, 'Lord, when did we see You hungry and feed You, or thirsty and give You drink? 38 When did we see You a stranger and take You in, or naked and clothe You? 39 Or when did we see You sick, or in prison, and come to You?' 40 And the King will answer and say to them, Assuredly, I say to you, inasmuch as you did it to one of the least of these My brethren, you did it to Me.' Matthew 25:34-40 "Therefore do not worry, saying, 'What shall we eat?' Or 'What shall we drink?' or 'What shall we wear?' For after All these things the Gentiles seek. For your heavenly Father knows that you need all these things. But seek first the kingdom of God and His righteousness, and all these things shall be added to you. Therefore do not worry about tomorrow, for tomorrow will worry about its own things. Sufficient for the day is its own trouble. Matthew 6:31-34

4. LION'S GATE—Mark 16:15-18

Community Outreach –Evangelism –Revival

Jesus rode through the Lion's Gate as He presented His life for the salvation of man—"Hosanna in the Highest." The Lion's Gate is the entrance by which Jesus comes into the heart of man. We have been given the Commission to go forth into all the world and preach the Gospel with great power and boldness. Proverbs 28:1 says "The righteous are bold as a lion."

And one of the elders said to me, "Stop weeping; behold, the Lion that is from the tribe of Judah, the Root of David, has overcome so as to open the book and its seven seals." Rev. 5:5. The Lion of the Tribe of Judah shall break every chain and give to us the victory again and again. Jesus is the chain breaker. The Lion's Gate shall break every chain in Intercession City and bring Deliverance and Revival back to the area which will spread throughout Florida, the nation and the world.

And He said to them, "Go into all the world and preach the gospel to every creature. He who believes and is baptized will be saved; but he who does not believe will be condemned. And these signs will follow those who believe: In My name they will cast out demons; they will speak with new tongues; they will take up serpents; and if they drink anything deadly, it will by no means hurt them; they will lay hands on the sick, and they will recover." Mark 16:15-18

5. **HEROD'S GATE—Isaiah 9:6-7; Isaiah 22:22**
    Government—City Incorporation/Municipality.

Herod's Gate represents the government of Intercession City. God wants to rule and reign in Intercession City. Isaiah 9:6 states that "The government will be upon His shoulder. And His name will be called Wonderful, Counselor, Mighty God, Everlasting Father, Prince of Peach. Of the increase of His government and peace there will be no end. We must pray and contend for the governmental gate of Intercession City (Seat of authority) that God would reign through righteous leaders in positions over our city. Herod was a notorious leader and although this gate in Jerusalem was not named after him, we are reminded of the consequences of ungodly leaders. When Herod killed the Disciple James, he went after Peter and had him arrested. But this time intercessory prayer went up for Peter and God sent an angel to rescue him. We must contend for righteous governmental leaders for Intercession City. Through intercessory prayer we must shut the gates of hell and open up the doors of Heaven and establish an altar. Isaiah 22:22: The key of the house of David I will lay on his shoulder; So, he shall open, and no one shall shut; And he shall shut, and no one shall open.

For unto us a Child is born,
Unto us a Son is given;
And the government will be upon His shoulder.
And His name will be called
Wonderful, Counselor, Mighty God,
Everlasting Father, Prince of Peace.

Of the increase of His government and peace
There will be no end,
Upon the throne of David and over His kingdom,
To order it and establish it with judgment and justice
From that time forward, even forever.
The zeal of the Lord of hosts will perform this. Isaiah 9:6-7
The key of the house of David
I will lay on his shoulder;
So he shall open, and no one shall shut;
And he shall shut, and no one shall open. Isaiah 22:22

6. DAMASCUS GATE—Isaiah 62:4-5
Market Place—Economy

Damascus was considered the trade center of its time. Since the City of Damascus was located at a strategic trade route, we chose Damascus to represent the Market Place Economy of Intercession City. Intercession City is strategically placed as the "Heart of Florida"—Measurably the very center of Florida. Currently Intercession City is an economically depressed area. Isaiah 62:4-5 declares that it shall no longer be termed Forsaken or Desolate but called Hephzibah (sought after) and Beulah (a land flowing with milk and honey.) We expect the economy to change and the City will Live Again and become a prosperous and thriving community as it was during Osie England's era.

You shall no longer be termed Forsaken
Nor shall your land any more be termed Desolate;
But you shall be called Hephzibah, and your land Beulah;
For the Lord delights in you,
And your land shall be married.

For as a young man marries a virgin,
So shall your sons marry you;
And as the bridegroom rejoices over the bride,
So shall your God rejoice over you. Isaiah 62:4-5

7. THE NEW GATE—Revelation. 21:5; Deuteronomy 6:10-12
Rebuilding—New Housing

Then He who sat on the throne said, "Behold, I make all things new." Rev. 21-5

The New Gate represents the New Intercession City. The condition of Intercession City was surveyed, and pictures were taken for historical purposes to show what Intercession City used to look like. Intercession City is about to change. All of the run-down buildings and homes will be replaced with new beautiful homes and subdivisions, apartment complexes, and landscaping including housing for the elderly. The Old Hotel will be restored. God has given Wesley a vision for a 12 story Hotel and Embassy Center. Each floor to be named after the 12 tribes of Israel. Can the dead bones and dead hearts live again? God said he would breath on His city and it will come alive. "INTERCESSIONS CITY LIVE AGAIN"

Then He who sat on the throne said, "Behold, I make all things new." And He said to me, "Write, for these words are true and faithful." Rev. 21:5

"So it shall be, when the Lord your God brings you into the land of which He swore to your fathers, to Abraham, Isaac, and Jacob, to give you large and beautiful cities Which you did not build, houses full of all good things, which you did not fill, hewn-out wells which you did not dig, vineyards and olive trees which you did not plant—when you have eaten and are full— then beware,

lest you forget the Lord who brought you out of the land of Egypt, from the house of bondage. Deuteronomy 6:10-12

8. **THE JAFFA GATE—Deut. 6:6-9; 2 Timothy 2:15**
Learning, Teaching & Training Center—Education

The Jaffa Gate leads to the Tower of David Museum, once Jerusalem's citadel and now a showcase of its history (learning center). We chose the Jaffa Gate for education since it leads to the Museum and historical learning center. It is important that Christian Schools and a Bible Training Center be established in Intercession City to provide Christian Education. And yes, as with the Tower of David Museum in Jerusalem, we must also preserve the history and legacy of Intercession City remembering what great things God has done there in the past. Deut. 6:6-9 states that we are to teach our children diligently throughout their days and their lives. Osie England, founder, was sent by God to raise up orphans, teaching them the Word of God to carry around the world for worldwide revival. And again, we shall see both young and old being taught the Word of God and being trained for end time revival.

"And these words which I command you today shall be in your heart. You shall teach them diligently to your children, and shall talk of them when you sit in your house, when you walk by the way, when you lie down, and when you rise up. You shall bind them as a sign on your hand, and they shall be as frontlets between your eyes. You shall Write them on the doorposts of your house and on your gates. Deuteronomy 6:6-9

Be diligent to present yourself approved to God, a worker who does not need to be ashamed, rightly dividing the word of truth. 2 Timothy 2:15

Apostolic Council and Leaders

In the center of the chart with the 8 gates and needs of Intercession City there is a circle representing the spiritual and governing body of the Hub or City. The Lord spoke that He would give Arabella 12 Intercessors that will help support the assignment of Intercession City (Spiritual Apostolic Council). He would show her who they were and instructed her not to choose based on familiarity. He said: "When I speak to them, He would have spoken to their hearts." This 12-member Spiritual Apostolic Council will undergird the rebuilding of Intercession City through prayer and intercession, and prophetic declaration, receiving strategic insight for the direction of the City.

In addition to the 12 Spiritual Apostolic Council the Lord has directed Wesley to choose 12 members in addition to himself as a governing board of directors for the 8 gates or needs of Intercession City. There will be an Apostolic Council consisting of Wesley and 12 men and women who will lead in the rebuilding of the walls and gates of Intercession City through a nonprofit pubic foundation. The nonprofit foundation will be the means for receiving contributions and grants in order to meet the 8 needs of the City and to preserve the City's Christian Heritage. Each area of need (8 Gates) will be represented by at least one Governmental Apostolic Council member to oversee his or her area of assignment. Just as different families took their places on the wall during Nehemiah's day for the rebuilding of their section of the wall.

10

STORIES FROM THE BOOK OF OSIE

Earlier we summarized the early life of Osie England, her salvation and call into the ministry. In this chapter we will include some excerpts from *The Book of Osie or The Life of Bishop Osie England* by Clarence Allison Maddy so that the reader can have a glimpse of the life of this saintly woman of faith and compassion.

Miss Osie's Pioneer Days in Ohio and West Virginia (Pages 21-24)

The call of God was heavy on Miss Osie England and she began to preach the message of Perfect Love in her community. After leaving the public school classroom as a teacher she rented a large house and opened her first Mission School in Massieville, Ohio. Soon a strong class of believers was organized. It would be a long story to relate in detail the marvelous experiences that she and her co-laborers enjoyed. Often she, with her older students, walked as far as five miles to carry on revival meetings in the adjacent communities. Everywhere she or her students set foot, the Lord blessed with a revival.

When Osie first started her ministry, her friends were few because they thought she had gone crazy over religion. However, after watching her steady progress, they saw God was with her and they became friends again plus there were many other new ones that the Lord gave her. Osie was very self-denying, but she had friends that would divide their last crust rather than see her want for anything. Many of her pupils began to feel a call as missionaries and evangelist. Fearing that their lack of experience might cause them to become discouraged, she closed the Mission School at the end of the third year to engage directly in Gospel work and conducted her first Camp Meeting at Piketon, Ohio. Somehow the man who lived nearest to where the canvas tabernacle was to be pitched got it into his mind that we were a bunch of noisy fanatics. Thus, before the meeting began or the tents were fully pitched, the mayor advised that we move two blocks below to what he said was a better location in the shade near a stream of water, rather than offend a citizen of the town. The sad part of it was, the man who tried to stop us fell dead while the meeting was in progress on the other side of town.

When we landed in the town, we were without money and without friends, so far as we knew. We did have a part sack of flour and the oven which belonged to an old oil stove. I built a furnace and my sisters, who were good cooks, tried to bake bread, but the smoke came the wrong way and covered the puffy loaves with a heavy coat of soot. Having spent most of the day in moving and in putting up the tents, we were very hungry. Miss Osie called us in for prayer, assuring us that God was able to send in the need. We had not prayed long until we arose with confidence. My ten-year-old brother who was visiting us in the camp looked out over the river bank and saw a large fish floundering in the shallow water on the other side. He hurriedly swam across and brought back the fish. About that time, the postmaster, who was a good Methodist in the town, sent his little daughter down with three loaves of bread which he said the Lord had commissioned him to send to the camp meeting. Later when we related to him how it was in direct answer to prayer, he furnished the bread for the rest of the camp and then wanted to provide it as we moved seventy miles to our next meeting. The spiritual pay he received was something for which we all thanked the Lord: His daughters became definitely established in the Lord, one of them now a great success as the wife of a minister; and we understand that Brother Leist (for that was the man's name) has now also entered the work of the ministry.

Miss Osie's experience as an educator gave her the ears of the cultured people, and for this reason her converts, which number into thousands, usually stand fast in the faith, since they are of the type who have stamina and a capacity for the grace and power of God.

The next camp meeting that summer was conducted in southern Ohio. Since money was scarce and the trip was a long one, we borrowed an express wagon and after hitching it behind the Model T Ford, limped off toward a faraway post. Long before we reached the destination, the wagon wheels turned turtle and left us stranded. We left the broken down vehicle and tenting by the roadside while we drove on in the old Ford to the campground. Through the kindness of a brother by the name of Allison, an uncle of the writer, the Ark of the Lord was carted safely to the journey's end.

This was a new chapter in the life of our former school teacher. Here, again, everything must be prayed down, including seats for the tabernacle, lights for the tents and meals for the workers. Again, God proved His promise to supply all our need, for instead of ordinary loaves, He sent great oversized mother-loaves, about fifteen inches long and instead of eggs of ordinary size, there were giant goose-eggs, which made a Benjamin's mess for the most festive-minded missionary among the group. We cannot go into detail about the refreshing revivals that followed. Nevertheless, events came, strengthened the idea that the Spirit was calling Miss Osie as He did Philip, to the farther Southland. Soon missions sprang up in the wake of the evangelistic campaigns. One of the most prominent of these was planted in Point Pleasant, West Virginia. Here her sister, Dora, sold her heating stove for fifteen dollars to pay the first month's rent on the Mission Building.

The furnishings were very humble. There were straw ticks on iron bedsteads with solid slats. The furniture was made of storeboxes. The cook stove was old and persisted in smoking, but here was not murmur from Miss Osie nor her workers. Here she found warm friends in the person of Brother and Sister Cheesebrew. Mr. Cheesebrew was chief of police in the town and while the Spirit worked on the souls of the people, he kept order among the unruly ones. Dozens of people stopped using liquor and tobacco and the lodge-goers, both among the men and women, found in Christ and His Church so much more than what they had experienced in their Secret Order that they started a midweek prayer meeting on the very night that they had once set aside for their fraternal order meetings.

The news of the great revival spread like wild fire and in a few weeks twenty calls for meetings lay on the desk at one time. To fill these calls was an impossibility without many new recruits. Accordingly, Miss Osie called her handful of faith workers to prayer in behalf of a Training School where young ministers and missionaries could be trained to enter the large, overripe harvest field. After much waiting before the Lord, The West Virginia Training School (Point Pleasant, WV) was founded by faith on Interdenominational lines. Truly the Lord watered this vine of His own planting with the very mercies of Heaven and from this small beginning, other institutions were soon operating in the Lord's Name.

The first session of the West Virginia Training School was in 1923-24 (during the time Interocean City, Florida was first being built), a three months' term with an enrollment of forty boys and girls who accepted training for missionary work at home and abroad. No charge was made for board, lodging or books. The curriculum was Bible, Missions, English, Practical Homiletics, General History, and a course in Visitation Work and in Street and Jail Services. Together the needs were prayed in.

There was an urgent need for chairs and tables for the school room. We did not know where they could come from, but we were taught to believe they would come. The next day there was rejoicing among us when the city baker drove up with his car top flat, for he had a stack of tables and chairs and he made several more trips to deliver all that gathered up. This man's little son, two and half years old, had been miraculously healed during that great revival and this the father's token of appreciation.

It was the writer's privilege to teach Bible and General History. One of the neighbors volunteered to teach Sight Reading in Music while Miss Osie taught the other subjects. Both morning and afternoon sessions were opened with a song and prayer. One afternoon as the classes were assembling, a worker entered and informed us that there was no bread for supper. In her prayer, Miss Osie told the Lord that we had neither bread nor money, but we were depending upon Him to supply all our needs. She became so absorbed in teaching that she forgot all about the bread. When school was dismissed at four o'clock, there was a knock at the kitchen door, and the cook called Miss Osie, who went immediately; and there she found a neighbor who was on his way home from where he worked at the Ship Building Plant. He took off his cap and apologized for his grimy face and hands and clothes. He said, "Please excuse my appearance, for I was working on the ship when the Lord impressed me to bring you some bread money. I did not wait to go home and clean up for I feared you might need it." He handed her three dollars. (At that time, bread sold six loaves for a quarter). Miss Osie received the offering with joy and told him the story. She said, "I know we did not pray loud enough for the neighbors to hear, it was truly the Lord that advised you."

Another of her friends contributed a quarter of a beef. When serving the last of it, Miss Osie remarked to the cook that she was glad that it lasted while the lady missionary was visiting us. She did not ask the Lord for more, but thanked Him for what had been provided. That same evening another quarter of a beef came in from a different source. So it was impressed upon the students that it pays to trust where we cannot see.

Miss Osie's Compassion for the Poor and the Orphans (pages 34-37)

When Miss Osie was called to give up her work as a public school teacher and enter the Gospel ministry, she had no intention of establishing child shelters for faith orphanages. Her definite burden was for the Home and Foreign Mission work. Nevertheless, because she retained her love for children, she soon found herself surrounded by unfortunate little ones, who by various means, had found their way to the different missions. Thus, before Miss Osie was aware of this added responsibility, she was rather astonished to find almost a dozen children that were all under sixteen years of age. Therefore, with automatic precision, the Point Pleasant Mission developed an important department which has come to be known as the Mountain State Orphanage.

For the benefit of you readers who will all likely be interested in the dependent children, we shall recite a few incidents concerning their entry. Among the scores of children who have been admitted to one of the Homes, there are some outstanding cases to which we shall briefly refer:

The Orphanage twins, who are known in mission circles as Johnnie and Jennie, have an almost preposterous story of rescue to their babyhood. When they were but seven weeks old, one of the local physicians called Miss Osie and told her that a mother, who lived about eight miles out in the county, was in a dying condition with leakage of the heart and that her twin babies could not survive much longer. He asked her to visit the home.

Two of the matrons went with Miss Osie, and although the red mud of the slippery clay road presented quite a hazard, the little Ford that carried the rescue party brought them to this scene of dire poverty. The only road leading to the two-room shack was a narrow cow path. The mother, in a weak voice, expressed her appreciation in advance for any help they could give.

It was not their intention to take the babies at that time, but to make the investigation; but when they saw the awful condition, they took off their coats, wrapped the babies in them and hurried back to the Orphanage quarters. Here they were laid on a blanket in front of the fire where they were bathed with water and then with oil. Day by day new signs of life and vigor began to demonstrate itself in the bodies and personalities of these little babies who were so emaciated that their bodies were a mass of wrinkles. They looked more like monkeys than like human beings.

They developed into beautiful children and when they were five years old, Jennie openly announced, as she drummed away on her toy ukulele, that she wanted to be a singing evangelist. Of course, she was going to be the song leader, chiefly because her twin brother, Johnnie, was called to be a preacher. They practiced day by day and had the other little tots for their audience.

It was about this time when the Mountain State Orphanage had to close down because the building was condemned, and we had to put up a fireproof structure. In the meantime, Johnnie and Jennie, along with other children, were placed in a boarding home by the State. When the Orphanage was open in the new building, the twins were still held in the custody of the State.

They are now in high school and last winter Miss Osie received a nice letter from them in which they told her they would like to have Bibles. Immediately, she purchased them each a lovely Bible which she mailed to them. They were very grateful and expressed their appreciation. The prayers of the mission workers still follow these precious children.

Time would fail us if we tried to relate even the extreme circumstances into which fate placed so many of these fatherless little ones who come under the observation of Miss Osie at both Orphanages. For instance, one little boy was so neglected that maggots were actually working in different places on his body. Another case was that of a little girl seventeen months old whose arms and legs hung like ropes. From lack of nourishment, she had developed rickets. The State left her with us until she matured into a beautiful, normal child and was placed in a home far away from all her relatives who had so shamefully neglected her.

Still another had legs as crooked as an Indian Chief's bow, but through prayer and some straight jacket bone-strengtheners, he can now stand as erect as a full-grown poplar. Most of the little ones at first shy at the sight of soap and water and wonder if the scouring they get is a punishment or a necessity; however, the matron does not attempt to get their little bodies clean with one bath, but follows up the bathing and the anointing with oil. One fourteen-year-old girl said that she never remembered of having but one bath in all her life.

Some years ago, Miss Osie and her workers spent Christmas Day in delivering baskets of food and clothing to poor families in and around Point Pleasant, West Virginia. She entered one home where she found the mother and eight children. The father was in jail, charged with bootlegging. The mother claimed that an enemy placed a bottle of liquor in their yard and then reported to the officers. In spite of the protest of innocency, the man was held in jail for further evidence.

The mother expressed her thanks and said they would now have a good Christmas dinner, but their cow was starving. She had fed her their last pumpkin. They needed the cow for milk, but she would sell her that day, if she could find a buyer. Miss Osie promised her that she would do what she could to secure some feed. All places of business were closed, but she phoned the sheriff and told him she had no appetite for a Christmas dinner until he found relief for that starving cow. The sheriff referred her to the man who owned the farm on which this tenant lived. She promptly contacted the owner and he promised to send a load of fodder out at once. Miss Osie visited the home again later in the day to make sure the cow was munching her feed.

Her attention was drawn to another needy family who lived at the edge of town. It was a rainy evening and she asked one of the young men from the Training School to go along and drive for her. They drove up in front of the dingy cottage and knocked on the front door when a voice from within called out, "Come around to the back door."

They went with their baskets around to the back and entered the kitchen where they found the parents and five children seated around the supper table. On each plate was a spoonful of granulated sugar and a piece of bread fried on top of the stove. They were dipping the bread in the sugar and eating it.

The house was leaking to the extent that the table and the beds were moved into the only dry spots left. After prayer, the mother explained that the father was almost blind due to emery dust in which he worked. Miss Osie was not satisfied with giving only temporary relief, but contacted an eye specialist over in Ohio who agreed to give the man free treatment, if she could get him over there. The mission paid his transportation twice a week for several weeks, after which his vision was restored and he was again able to work. In the meantime, the mission supplied their food.

A major factor in the disposition of Miss Osie which contributes to her general success is her working spirit and courage. Even before she entered mission work, while she was teaching in the public school, the writer saw her walk bravely through a crowd of furious rioters and call their names one by one as she passed among them. Although she knew there were rifles, corn cutters and other firearms involved in the melee, she, by her presence, shamed the insurrectionist until they stealthily slipped away without becoming involved in the bloodshed that they had purposed.

Miss Osie Loved Christians of all Denominations (Pages 44-45, 56)

Although Miss Osie's former church denomination was Presbyterian, and her present affiliation is with the Household of Faith Movement (Wesleyan Methodist), she has remained Interdenominational with a benediction of God-speed for the Christians of all churches.

Her experiences in the educational field and her spirit of humiliation in holding up Christ have drawn to her standard the very cream of Christianity from every walk of life. She shows no distinction between the illiterate and the college-bred of potentate extraction. Her doctrine is: God's Grace is sufficient to bring the down-and-out up, and the up-and-down to the common level of full salvation by faith through Christ. Since she has labored untiringly without stipulated salary for more than thirty-five years, her loyal co-laborers are stepping out on the same platform. Many of these called-out Christians have already entered the vocation of soul-saving in many churches.

When it comes to attire, Miss Osie has no changeable suits of apparel which need be salted down in moth balls and the like. Neither is she of the type of a certain missionary that the writer heard of who had fourteen hats and seventeen pairs of shoes at one time. The plain garb in which Miss Osie and many of her helper array themselves never goes out of style, because blue uniforms and black hose have not been in style recently and, therefore cannot go out.

During the days when it was taking every penny to build and furnish the Orphanages, she made one pair of shoes last several years. This was possible because she had a friend who half-soled shoes for the mission workers without charge.

One of the great reasons that Miss Osie has been able to accomplish so much with so little money is because she never wastes a dollar or spends a nickel needlessly. When one sends his tithe and offering to the Lord's treasury at one of the orphanages or missions, none of it goes for salaries or superfluities. Thus, it is easy to pray for the actual needs, for the Lord always has someone somewhere that responds in the moment of testing.

Miss Osie still walks by faith and has no bank stock. The extraordinary gift of government is more than a natural trait or even something that has been cultivated through her years of active diplomacy, the schoolroom, the pulpit, council chamber and her other appearances as a public supervisor of organizations and institutions.

Many of these co-laborers have dedicated themselves in the same fashion with Miss Osie and wear the plainest of clothes and thrive on common food and depend upon God to supply their financial, physical and spiritual needs. They are not radical or fanatical, except in matters pertaining to sin and worldliness. Her conciliatory attitude toward the Christians of all churches has given her co-workers a like desire to live peaceably with all men and, by becoming all things, win a few and help edify those who are already the Lord's sheep, regardless of the separate folds with which circumstances, environment and education have caused them to become thus affiliated. Most of the workers are poor in the world's goods, but you can't buy them with pleasure, office or money.

Miss Osie and her corps of Christian agents desire to hold Christ up wherever there is an open door. They always work interdenominationally and do not proselyte or cater to Christian professors who are addicted to that shameful practice. Her slogan is: "CHRIST FOR EVERY SOUL'S CRISIS"! She teaches that there is no case too hard for Him.

To name all of Miss Osie's co-laborers and the part they play would fill a book that would take a lifetime to write.

Tears for Worldwide Revival

Throughout *The Book of Osie* we see the heart of Miss Osie to be much larger than the regions of the states from which she conducted her ministries. Osie's heart was to the State, to the Nation, and to the World. As mentioned earlier she longed and wept for the salvation of souls throughout the State of Florida, the Nation and for worldwide revival—Pages 53 and 68.

As mentioned in Chapter 2 history teaches that every great revival or religious reform has come about by extraordinary agony and burden-bearing.

It has been said that Miss Osie shed more tears over the lost than any other Christian woman since the days of the wailing women of Jerusalem and the weeping prophet. It is no wonder that Osie's prayers moved the Hand of God for worldwide revival.

Ministry Centers were Springing up in Florida

"The thing that blesses Miss England most about new Centers springing up in the Sunshine State is not only the warmth and health for the physical bodies, but the Heavenly Sunshine which beams down from the devotional and spiritual singing, praying and preaching series. Two of the questions that they ask (in regard to the Centers) are:

First, will the huge Grace Bowl Temple which is being planned for the evangelizing of all Florida and all other state tourists be a factor in the revival which the world so much needs?

Second, will the Biblical College, which has already begun to show prospects of a spiritual school, fill a need that will assist to curb the juvenile delinquency in Florida and other states?

Ministry Center at Fellowship Front in Sanford, Florida: More than a quarter of a million dollars was spent in preparing over five hundred and fifty rooms for the Lord's people who had gathered from thirty-five different denominations and forty one states. In addition Fellowship Front housed three hundred and eighty-five widows, missionaries, ministers and other retiring Christian people. At Fellowship Front Miss England and the other Christian leaders and laity organized around the clock twenty-four-hour-a-day prayer meetings—Page 57.

11

AUTHOR'S CONNECTION TO INTERCESSION CITY

Wesley J. Weaver
Author of Intercession City Lives Again

Arabella A. Weaver, Author's wife
Apostolic Intercessor to Intercession City

Lawrence & Lillian Weaver
Wesley's mother and father.

Many of you may be asking how Wesley and Arabella Weaver became connected to this once beautiful city of God. It is a long story and we shall capture only a portion of it here. Actually, Arabella and I met in Intercession City by Divine Providence. The full story will be told in our next publication "Unity Marries the Land" by Wesley and Arabella Weaver.

My parents named me Wesley James Weaver after the great Methodist Evangelist John Wesley. My story of Intercession City is relatively new. The story begins during the summer of 2016, when I was 72 years old. After 48 years of marriage to my faithful and loving wife, Nan departed this earth to be with Jesus in Heaven on March 10, 2016, leaving behind four children, nine grandchildren and myself. I contemplated what was next in my life and began to diligently seek the Lord. I told the Lord that I would stay single and give the rest of my life to Him. I cried out for souls and after reading of great men and women of faith, longed for signs, miracles, healings and revival. In May 2016, the Lord spoke that I would remarry, and the following July appeared in a vision just after midnight that He was going to give me what I asked. That same summer after my wife's departure I was visiting with my sister in Geneva, Alabama. She had inherited our father's photo album and asked: "Have you ever seen dad's photo album? I responded: "No, I have never *seen* my dad's photos." I was so fascinated that I scanned the entire album so that I could have my own photo album of my dad. You see, the last time I saw my father was around 1949 when I was around five years of age. After that he moved to California and I never saw him since. He died in California in 1989.

For the first time in my life I saw pictures of myself, my mom, dad, brother and sister in Intercession City when we lived there from 1945 to 1948. Now, I have always heard the story about us living in Intercession City and at the age of three vaguely remember the place but was told I almost died there from malaria and malnutrition. So, all my life until last year my thoughts were: Oh, my dad from Marion, Ohio must have been a sucker. Perhaps he read an ad in the newspaper "Cheap land in Florida" and perhaps bought that 5-acre parcel of mosquito infested land sight unseen. But that is not what happened. During the summer of 2016, I was browsing through my dad's photo album and I discovered some strange photos I never paid much attention to before. Several photos show a group of people traveling from Point Pleasant, West Virginia, to Intercession City, Florida in 1935. The automobiles and trucks were from the 1930s. The captions below the old photos were "Going to Florida on School Bus 1935. Arrive in Florida from West Virginia 1935." Next, came photos of a vacant two-story building with archways surrounded by weeds. And finally, a picture of my father, Lawrence

Weaver, in front of a palm tree with the caption "First time to Florida 1935." I was elated that my dad on most all of his photos had dated and identified each photo. I looked at the photos of the vacant two-story building with arches and read: "Osie England Bible School Intercession City, Florida 1935. Hotel at Intercession City, Florida 1935." Thoughts flooded my mind: Who in the world is Osie England? Why was my dad with this group of people and what about the pictures of the hotel and Osie England Bible School? I began to research the internet to see if I could gather any information. I entered into my search block Intercession City. It did not take long in discovering Ted LaVigne's website "Historic Intercession City." What an eye opener for me. I devoured everything the late historian Ted LaVigne placed on his site about the history of Osie England and Intercession City. Then I began to discover my roots and the missing story of my father's early life and connection to Osie England and Intercession City. At age 72 I was able to put together the missing pieces of my early life in Intercession City and that of my father's life with Osie England from Point Pleasant, West Virginia to Intercession City, Florida, being one of the pioneer families. I shall always be thankful and grateful to Ted for his research of Osie England and his posting of the history of Intercession City on his website, without which I would not be where I am today in Intercession City writing this story.

After discovering Ted Lavigne's website during the summer of 2016, I reached out to him using an email posted on his website. I never received a response and assumed he was too busy or not interested in my findings and photos of Intercession City. Unbeknownst to me I was using a discontinued email and Ted never received my inquiry. The following December, several months later I felt that perhaps I should try again to contact Ted. With a little research I was able to find a good email address and reached out to him sending him some of the pictures of Intercession City from my dad's album. I received a response right away and he was happy to see the photos and hear my story. As fellow historians we became close friends. A few weeks later in December just after Christmas my sister and I visited Ted and he showed us all around Intercession City pointing out the landmarks and telling the history. After first meeting Ted we bonded immediately. We had a lot in common—Both of us being spirit filled senior citizens having spent most all of our lives in the ministry, and both of us having a consuming desire for revival and the study of great men and women of faith we shared many happy moments together.

We do not know how my father met Osie England in Point Pleasant, West Virginia nor his position with the various ministries established there—church, orphanage, missionary training school, etc.—whether a staff member, a student, or a worker. We do know that my father grew up in Ohio not far from Osie England and his family had connections with the Wesleyan faith. My father's oldest brother and his wife were Methodist, and both attended Ohio Wesleyan University. Osie held many Camp Meeting Revival services throughout Ohio and I would assume my father attended one of her Tabernacle meetings and perhaps became a born-again believer through her ministry. Practically all of her staff members originated from Ohio. As you can observe on the map, Point Pleasant lies on the West Virginia side of the Ohio River near southern Ohio not far from the Columbus, Ohio area where Osie and my father grew up.

Current site (where trees are located) of the five acres off Wooten Road, Intercession City, Florida purchased by Wesley's father from Osie England where a log home was constructed. Wesley lived here until 1947 (Age three)

Pictures taken in 1935 when Wesley's father left Point Pleasant, WV in 1935 with the second caravan of families and children. After Osie England secured the 5,000 acres of land and buildings in Interocean City in 1934, she left a small contingent of her staff there and returned to Point Pleasant with most of her remaining party in order to arrange for the relocation of her ministry headquarters to Florida. These pictures show the group leaving Point Pleasant, WV and arriving in Florida. Included in the pictures is how the old abandoned hotel looked before it was turned into a Bible training center (Osie England Bible School and later named Intercession Institute).

Left: Pumping up the tire from the long drive from Point Pleasant, WV to Interocean, Florida. They traveled the Old Dixie Highway. Right: Wesley's father Lawrence Weaver. First time to Florida 1935

Lawrence Weaver arrives in Intercession City in 1935. Picture taken at the old abandoned hotel when he first arrived in 1935.

Lawrence house I built in Pensacola Fla do War II 1941

During World War II my father met my mother, Lillian Myrtle Gray of Pensacola, Florida, through the Lonely Hearts Club and moved from Intercession City to Pensacola. They were married and bore three children in succession, Margaret, Larry, and me. We lived next door to my mother's sister and husband, Jim and Martha Brock. Supplies were short during the war and many things were rationed. However, my father was able to obtain cinder blocks and build a home where we resided until the end of the war. See captioned photo "Lawrence house I built in Pensacola, Fla—War II 1941.

At the close of the War my father decided to return to Intercession City. He purchased five acres of land from Osie England, purchased a tent, where they lived until he completed his log home. This picture captioned "Our first step in building home—Weavers home in Intercession City, Fla." It was at this stage of construction in 1947 (two room house with no running water or bathroom) when I contracted Malaria and became malnourished and almost died. The Lord woke up my aunt in Pensacola to go to Intercession City and check on the children. She and my uncle arrived just in the nick of time to save me. My father had backslid and became involved in palm reading and the occult. He was working long hours out of town to make money to support his family and build his home. My mother had a nervous breakdown and neglected us. The older siblings took my milk and I became very frail and malnourished.

My father was also an artist. To the right you will see one of his paintings in front of the log home captioned "One of my art pictures—Lawrence H Weaver 1938." As a young child I remember seeing a painting he did of Jesus coming in the clouds of Glory upon His second return.

Wesley and his brother Larry Weaver sitting on their Dad's scooter (Wesley seated in front of his older brother). The beginning of the construction of the log home their father was building on the five acres of land purchased from Osie England in Intercession City.

First, second, & third stages of construction of log home on Wooten Road, Intercession City, Florida

Fourth, fifth and sixth stages of construction of log home on Wooten Rd. Intercession City. As you can see the end results turned out rather attractive. However, the completion came two years after my aunt and uncle took us to Pensacola (1947)

This picture was taken by my father in 1945, ten years after my father's arrival in Intercession City. The hotel was turned into Osie England's Bible School and later renamed Intercession Institute.

My father's trade was in construction and painting. As a commercial painter he painted a number of prominent buildings (churches, schools, etc.) and smoke stacks in this area of Florida. On one of his jobs he fell painting a 75-foot smoke stack and crushed both ankles.

We also know from the photo album that my father was a builder and a painter. There were two photos in the album of a home he built in Pensacola during WWII and another home built in Intercession City on five acres of land purchased from Osie England. When my father and the other members of Miss Osie England's group arrived in Intercession City during the winter of 1935, the buildings were in bad repair. As you can see from my dad's photos the weeds were tall and as described the old hotel needed much repair having been vacant for ten years. it is believed my father among others in the group from West Virginia helped Osie England repair and rebuild many of the structures in Intercession City that were in ruin after being vacated for a decade.

My father, Lawrence Weaver, was not with the first party that came down to Interocean City in 1934. That group only consisted of Osie England, Clarence Maddy, several staff members and about 40 orphans. After Osie England and Clarence Maddy secured the 5,000 acres and buildings in Interocean City for an orphanage, they were unable to obtain a permit from the State of Florida for the run-down hotel. Therefore, most of the party with the orphans returned to Point Pleasant during the spring of 1935, leaving 5 adults and 7 youth to maintain the property.

The following year in 1935, a caravan of staff members, their families, and workers departed Point Pleasant for Interocean City, my father being among them, as captured in his photo album. While in Intercession City my father remained single during the construction years and rebuilding of Intercession City. Then the War years came from 1939 to 1945 (World War II) which took many young men into service and others left for factories to produce war equipment and supplies. Shortages and rationing made things difficult here, however Intercession City and Osie England's ministries continued without interruption in spite of the War.

At this time my father in his early thirties was looking for a wife and with the help of the Lonely Heart's organization he found a Southern Bell living in Pensacola, Florida by the name of Lillian Myrtle Gray. They began to write each other and before long my dad moved to Pensacola and married my mom. Three children were born in close succession, I, being the last was born in 1944. We resided in Pensacola throughout the remainder of World War II.

After the war ended my dad wanted to move back to Intercession City, buy some land, and build a house for his family. My dad visited Intercession City in 1945 and on September 10, 1946, he purchased 5 acres of land from Miss Osie England. We did not have a car because my dad loaned his car to someone and they wrecked it, so we all took the bus to Intercession City. The first thing was to purchase a scooter to get around and a tent for his family of five to live in until the log cabin was built. It was very remote. Only one other family lived in that area—the Wootens. So, we lived in a tent until such time my dad could build his log house. My dad bought logs from the local saw mill owned by the president of the Bible College—Mr. A.J. Smith and started building his log house. He obtained employment painting smoke stacks and other commercial property. On one job he fell 75 feet and broke both ankles.

Dad would work long hours and get home late. In his spare time, he worked on building the house. But this cost his family dearly. Because of the primitive conditions my mother had a nervous breakdown. My mom and dad sometimes had fights. The well was not dug and the only water we had was in a large barrel we kept near the house. We had to get water from the Wootens and many times there were mosquito larvae in the water we had to use to drink, cook, and bath with. We had no bathrooms inside or outside—not even an outhouse. I remember having to go to the side of the house to use the bathroom. All three of the children were being neglected; and, since I was the youngest being two years of age, my older siblings would steal my milk because none of us had enough food to eat. The milk in my bottle was often sour and curdled. I would scrounge through the garbage to find a peanut butter lid with a little peanut butter on it. I became malnourished and contracted malaria. My mom was acting strange and someone passing through reported us to the authorities.

One night God woke up my aunt in Pensacola in the middle of the night and said, "Go check on the kids." That morning they immediately got into the car and drove from Pensacola to Intercession City. When they found me, I was almost at the point of death from malnutrition and malaria. They took me to the doctor. The doctor said I would not live but God had a plan for my life and against all odds recovered. If my aunt and uncle from Pensacola had not come when they did all three of us would have become wards of the state. The state authorities were about to step in and take us away. My mother was committed to the mental hospital in Chattahoochee and my dad eventually moved to California where he lived the rest of his life.

My aunt and uncle became our legal guardians and gave us a wonderful Christian home. We moved to the country outside Pensacola on a 40-acre farm in a small community named Beulah. They took great care of us and took us to Beulah Baptist Church every time the doors were open—Sunday morning, Sunday night, Wednesday nights, and during revival services. Most every service we would sing "Beulah Land." I accepted the Lord at the age of 12 during a revival service and later during my military service in Germany accepted the call into the ministry at the age of 21, later receiving my Bachelor of Theology degree at Liberty Bible College in Pensacola, Florida and afterwards serving my local church and related ministries as an elder, pastor, board member, treasurer, etc. including seven years as the Accountant for the Brownsville Revival.

For the past fifty years I served both in the church and the marketplace, holding positions as Accounting Supervisor at the Naval Air Station, Auditor for State of Florida, Controller for two different colleges, and having my own accounting and tax firm—Northwest Florida Consultants specializing in nonprofit organizations, ministers and missionary tax returns.

12

CONCLUSION

In conclusion I believe the following prayer request article titled "Things to Pray About" from the *Defender of the Faith, Volume III, Pt. Pleasant, W. Va., December, 1923*, gives us a glimpse into the heart of this great woman of God who undoubtedly had the Heart of God for the world.

THINGS TO PRAY ABOUT

1. *A Mother's wayward son at Middleport, Ohio.*
2. *A young man up the Kanawha Valley who sent an offering to the Mission Thanksgiving but who is unsaved.*
3. *A young man who is saved, but whose father forbids him coming to the Training school.*
4. *A young man from the state of Georgia who had planned to come to the Training School but could not because of lack of funds. His father has suffered crop failure for several successive years.*
5. *A cow for the Training home that our girls who are already overworked may have fresh milk.*
6. *Money to meet the running expenses of the school and to pay the notes as they fall due.*
7. *Comfortable chairs with wide arms for the students to use.*
8. *A meek and humble spirit for each teacher and pupil in the Training School.*

Osie England and theIntercessors Were...

R O P E H O L D E R S

The word "Ropeholders" means much to the students of I.C.B.C.; this is the name of the student missionary prayer band. The group meets each week in behalf of missions, both at home and abroad.

Many of the Ropeholders have bidden the group farewell and are now actively engaged in the work of reaching those "On the Darker Side of the Road," while many others plan to be leaving soon.

It is the belief of this group that "holding the ropes" by means of intercessory prayer is an important part of missionary work. We of the group intend to be "Ropeholder Missionaries" until we hear the command, "Go ye."

This collage of photos displayed on the back wall of the Community Wesleyan Church in Intercession City shows some of the missionaries sent out all over the world under Osie England's ministry: Ethiopia, Egypt, New Guina, Cuba, Haiti, India, and Native Americans, to name a few.

INTERCESSION CITY IN THE PAST

INTERCESSION CITY IN THE FUTURE

INTERCESSION CITY LIVES NOW—
THE MOVEMENT IS NOW!

The 24/7-100 DAY Prayer Revival TENT started on Passover Sunday, April 21st–July 30th, 2019. God said, gather the Intercessors, tell them to come, cover twelve hours shifts or what they could to intercede for His City to Live Again. He said the enemy's time was up. The seventy years of captivity of His City was over and He wanted it back. He wanted His City to Live Again. As Intercessors we knew we were there to Plow the Ground, to reverse the curse that had held the City in captivity, and prepare it for the Apostle and Evangelist to build and multiply. Much like in Bishop Osie England days they came from far and near, throughout Florida and as far as Texas, Oklahoma, and Louisiana. Many came,they said, to help put their Prayer time into re-digging wells and to be a part of the history of rebuilding the walls of God's City, Intercession City.

This TENT for a 100 Days was a place of Revival to the lost and wandering. It brought Peace, Safety, Comfort and Rescue...and lives were impacted. It was protected by the Community—much was donated and nothing was stolen. Angels were seen standing guard, Gold Dust on chairs, and Rainbows accompanied visitors in their cars while driving. Writings in the sky were a blessing ("Jesus 4 Gives"—"Thank U Jesus"), and prophetic messages were left by the unknown passing through. We survived the seasonal "lovebugs", the mosquitoes, and smothering summer heat. The TENT weathered the July storms, winds, flooding rains; and through it all, the presence of God left a mark on the City that hungers for more. "When is the TENT going back up?" the City characters asked—the community wanted to know..."Soon" we replied, "Soon." It came down temporary to only search for a new location in Intercession City. The Intercessors came and Plowed well. In Oneness, John 17, the only way. But this was ONLY just the beginning, Only the

Beginning. God said, "Now Souls salvation, come forth into God's City, the state, the nation, and the Kingdom." Stay tuned in...

Decree for Intercession City

The following DECREE was compiled by Intercessors throughout Florida for Intercession City to LIVE AGAIN. It was read and decreed daily during the 100 DAY Prayer Revival under the Tent from April 21 through July 30, 2019, in Intercession City.

John 17:21 Father God we come to You as one in Christ, as one with You Father, and as one with one another for Your plan, Your call, Your purpose upon Intercession City.

Psalm 24:7 We cry out, "Lift up your heads, O you gates; be lifted up you everlasting doors; and the King of glory shall come in, 24:8 Who is this King of glory? The Lord strong and mighty, the Lord mighty in battle. We open the gates to Intercession City to usher in the King of Glory.

Ezra. 4:3 We Your people are building a house of prayer in Intercession City unto the Lord our God. 4:4 Our hands are strong to build and we shall not be troubled in the building of this city. 4:5 There shall be no counselors hired against us to cause trouble in the re-building of Intercession City nor to frustrate God's purpose. 4:12 We are setting up the walls and joining the foundation. Ezra 5:5 We decree that the work shall not cease for Your eye, O God is upon this work. 5:11 We are the servants of You, Father God of heaven and earth. We are re-building the house that was built these many years ago. 5:12 But after the house was built our fathers sinned and provoked the God of heaven and the house of prayer was destroyed and the people scattered. 5:13 But Father repentance for the sin of Intercession City has been granted and the order to build again was given in the year of 2017. Ezra 6:1 Father the records have been searched and the original purpose and call upon Intercession City made known. Now Father according to

Your call upon Intercession City, Amos 9:11 We thank You for raising up the tabernacle of David that was fallen and closing-up the breaches. Father, we thank You for building it as in the days of old. 9:14 Father, we thank you for bringing again Your people to Intercession City, and that they are rebuilding this city. 9:15 Father, we thank You for planting them upon this land and that they shall no more be pulled out of this land which You have given to them.

Ezra 6:5 Heavenly Father, we thank You that all treasures removed from this city are being restored and brought again to the house of prayer in Intercession City. 6:8 We thank You Father that all provision needed for the completion of the House of Intercession is being supplied so that the work not be hindered. 6:10 That sacrifices of praise and petition, of sweet savors of sacrifice be made unto You, God of Heaven and earth. 6:12 That Your Name shall forever dwell here. 6:22 Lord, thank you for making us joyful and for turning those in authority unto us to strengthen our hands in the work of the house of God.

Isa.60:1 Intercession City! Arise! Shine! for your light has come and the glory of the Lord is risen upon you. 2b the Lord shall arise upon you. 3. the people have come to your light and officials to the brightness of your rising. (they shall come to see what is happening here in Intercession City).

Isa 61:2 We proclaim this is the acceptable year of the Lord. 61:3 Intercession City is the planting of the Lord, that He might be glorified. 61:4 We are building the old waste places and raising up the former desolations, we are repairing this wasted city, the desolation of 70 years. We, Your builder, are called priests of the Lord, ministers of our God. 61:7 Intercession City, for your shame you shall receive double honor. 61:8 We thank You, Lord God, that You are directing this work in truth. 61:10 We, Your builders, greatly rejoice in the Lord, our souls are joyful in our God. 61:11 The Lord is causing righteousness and praise to spring forth from Intercession City.

Isa,62:3 You, Intercession City is a crown of glory in the hand of the Lord and a royal diadem in the hand of our God. 62:4 You are no longer termed Forsaken; neither your land be termed Desolate: but you, Intercession City, is called Hepzibah (for the Lord delights in you) and your land Beulah (married). We decree this Land to be a land of prosperity flowing with milk and honey! The Lord delights in you, Oh Intercession City and your land is now married.

62:5 Our God rejoices over you! Matt. 21:13 as He decrees, MY HOUSE, INTERCESSION CITY, SHALL BE CALLED A HOUSE OF PRAYER!

Made in the USA
Columbia, SC
11 December 2021